THE FIDELITY OF BETRAYAL

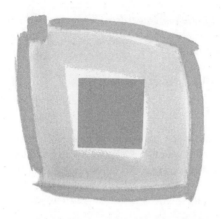

THE FIDELITY OF BETRAYAL
TOWARDS A CHURCH BEYOND BELIEF
PETER ROLLINS

Author of *How (Not) to Speak of God*

PARACLETE PRESS
Brewster, Massachusetts

The Fidelity of Betrayal: Towards a Church Beyond Belief

2008 First Printing

ISBN: 978-1-55725-560-0

Library of Congress Cataloging-in-Publication Data

Rollins, Peter.
  The fidelity of betrayal : towards a church beyond belief / Peter
  Rollins.
      p. cm.
  Includes bibliographical references.
  ISBN 978-1-55725-560-0
  1. God (Christianity) 2. Negative theology–Christianity. 3. Church
renewal. 4. Non-institutional churches. I. Title.
  BT103.R65 2008
  230–dc22   2008006181

10 9 8 7 6 5 4 3 2 1

Published by Paraclete Press
Brewster, Massachusetts
www.paracletepress.com

Printed in the United States of America

For my friends who know what it is to embrace their faith
by betraying it with a kiss.

CONTENTS

PROLOGUE
PROLOGUE

The Caretaker's Trial

There was once a small town filled with believers who sought to act always in obedience to the voice of God. When faced with difficult situations the leaders of the community would often be found deep in prayer, or searching the Scriptures for guidance and wisdom.

Late one evening, in the middle of winter, a young man from the neighboring city arrived at the gates of the town's little church seeking refuge. The caretaker immediately let him in and, seeing that he was hungry and cold, provided a meal and some warm clothes. After he had eaten, the young man explained how he had fled the city because the authorities had labeled him a political dissident. It turned out that the man had been critical of both the government and the church in his work as a journalist. The caretaker brought the young man back to his home and allowed him to stay until a plan had been worked out concerning what to do next.

When the priest was informed about what had happened, he called the leaders of the town together in order to work out what ought to be done. After an intense discussion it was agreed that the man should be handed over to the authorities in order to face up to the charges that had been made against him. But the caretaker protested, saying, "This man has committed no crimes, he has merely criticized what he believes to be the injustices perpetrated by authorities in the name of God."

"What you say may be true," replied the priest, "but his presence puts the whole of this town in danger. What if the authorities find out where he is and learn that we protected him."

But the caretaker refused to hand him over to the priest, saying, "He is my guest, and while he is under my roof I will ensure that no harm comes to him. If you take him from me by force then I will publicly attest to having helped him and suffer the same injustice as my guest."

The caretaker was well loved by the people, and the priest had no intention of letting something happen to him. So the leaders went away again and this time searched the Scriptures for an answer, for they knew that the caretaker was a man of deep faith. After a whole night of poring over the Scriptures the leaders came back to the caretaker, saying, "We have read the sacred book all through the night seeking guidance and found that it tells us that we must respect the authorities of this land and witness to the truth of faith through submission to them."

But the caretaker also knew the sacred words of Scripture, and he told them that the Bible also asked that we care for those who suffer and are persecuted. There and then the leaders began to pray fervently. They beseeched God to speak to them, not as a still small voice in their conscience, but rather in the way that he had spoken to Abraham and Moses. They begged that God would communicate directly to them and to the caretaker so that the issue could finally be resolved. Sure enough, the sky began to darken, and God descended from heaven, saying, "The priest and elders speak the truth, my friend. In order to protect the town this man must be handed over to the authorities."

The caretaker, a man of deep faith, looked up to heaven and replied, "If you want me to remain faithful to you, my God, then I can do nothing but refuse your advice. For you have already demanded that I look after this man. You have written that I must protect him at all costs. Your words of love have been spelled out by the lines of this man's face, your text is found in the texture of his flesh. And so, my God, I defy you precisely so as to remain faithful to you."

With this God smiled and quietly withdrew, confident that the matter had finally been settled.

INTRODUCTION
INTRODUCTION

What Would Judas Do?

I n the 1990s the phrase "What Would Jesus Do?"
became a popular slogan for millions of Christians
across the English-speaking world. Originally inspired by
the book *In His Steps* by Charles Sheldon, these words were
quickly reduced to the abbreviation "WWJD" and etched
onto countless bracelets as a way of reminding the bearer
that they held Jesus up as the ultimate authority in moral,
political, and religious matters. These bracelets quickly
became a popular accessory among Christian teenagers,
so much so that the letters "WWJD" started to appear on
a whole range of consumerist products such as jewelry,
bumper stickers, badges, bookmarks, key rings, and even
underwear.[1]

Of the various predictable parodies that arose in the
aftermath of this widespread phenomenon, there was one
that struck me as particularly intriguing and insightful. The
parody in question came to my attention via a Web site that
playfully offered the following advice: "When life throws

you a curveball, remember to just ask yourself: what would Judas do?"Although the actual intention of the Web site was superficial and satirical in tone (carrying mock testimonies of people who had considered this question and then gone on to lie, steal, and seduce), I was struck at the time by the thought that, far from offering some amoral, antireligious sentiment, the question "What Would Judas Do?" could perhaps offer us a tantalizing hint of what it would mean to ask, "What Would Jesus Do?"

In other words, what would Jesus do when confronted with Christianity today? Would Jesus do what Judas did, and betray it? In saying this I am not hinting at the rather mundane insight that Jesus would betray the anemic, inauthentic, self-serving Churchianity that so often festers quietly under the banner of Christianity today. I am not asking whether Jesus would turn the tables on what passes as contemporary Christianity in favor of a more robust and radical version that may have once existed in an age long past. Rather, by asking whether Jesus would betray Christianity as Judas betrayed Christ, I am asking if Jesus would plot the downfall of Christianity in every form that it takes. Or rather, to be more precise, I am asking whether Christianity, in its most sublime and revolutionary state, always demands an act of betrayal from the Faithful. In short, is Christianity, at its most radical, always marked by a kiss, forever forsaking itself, eternally at war with its own manifestation.

Such thinking leads to the seemingly paradoxical idea that the deepest way in which we can demonstrate our fidelity to

Christianity is to engage in a betrayal of it. If this is the case then, in order to remain true to the spirit of "WWJD" (the desire to emulate the life of Christ) we must inscribe the "J" with an ambiguous double meaning, one that simultaneously references both Jesus and Judas, one that dances between the two, one that cannot separate them any more than we can pry apart the "two" sides of a Möbius strip.

In order to explore this idea the following work is split into three complementary sections. The first explores what we mean by the idea of the Word of God, the second interrogates the Being of God, and the third introduces the reader to the centrality of the Event of God. As the book progresses, it will become clear that the Word, Being, and Event of God are inextricably bound up with each other in a Trinitarian structure that defies any attempt at being divided.

As this structure is gradually revealed, I argue that the consequences are twofold. First, we are led to embrace the idea of Christianity as a religion without religion, that is, as a tradition that is always prepared to wrestle with itself, disagree with itself, and betray itself. Second, this requires a way of structuring religious collectives that operate at a deeper level than the mere affirmation of shared doctrines, creeds, and convictions. It involves the formation of dynamic, life-affirming collectives that operate, quite literally, beyond belief.

On a personal note, the potentially controversial nature of this book has meant that there were times when I wondered whom I was really hoping to address with it. While staring out my window between words, there were times when I reflected upon who would pick up this book, read its message, and take it to heart. Indeed, I even had a dream one evening in which I witnessed my anonymous reader entering a library and, hesitating for a moment, slowly picking up the finished piece. Only now, as I re-read what I have written, have I finally worked out who it is I am writing to, only now have I worked out who that stranger in my dream really was, who it has always been: it has never been anyone other than myself. Just as the psychoanalyst Jacques Lacan once made the comment that a letter always reaches its destination, a book like this can never fail to reach the one to whom it is written. Why? For no other reason than because it is the one who writes it who is the intended reader.

In realizing this, I am reminded of a story in which a group of prophets pack their few belongings, bid farewell to their loved ones, and sail off to a faraway land in order to share their sacred message of salvation. After months of struggling with the stormy seas, often cursing their vocation for leading them into such terror and torment, they finally land on a sandy beach along the coastline of a distant country. Ravaged by starvation, doubt, and ill health, the now diminished group finally reaches a small city nestled inland and begins to preach. Being strangers, the group initially attracts a great deal of attention, and the people listen eagerly to their message. But as the weeks run into months and the months dissolve into years, the citizens finally stop taking any notice of these prophets in their midst. Yet still they enter the city each day and still they share their sacred message of joy and suffering. Eventually one of the inhabitants, who has become intrigued once more by the strangers, approaches them while no one is watching and asks, "Why do you continue to sing your sorrowful song when it is obvious that no one is listening anymore?" In response, one of the group steps forward, looks the young man in the eyes and, with deep tenderness, replies, "In those early days we spoke because we believed that we had something to share with the people of this land. But now, now we speak only to challenge ourselves to remain faithful to that to which we are bound."

Christianity is not brain surgery or rocket science, it is not quantum mechanics or nuclear physics; it is both infinitely easier and more difficult than all of these. The fragile flame of faith is fanned into life so simply: all we need do is sit still for a few moments, embrace the silence that engulfs us, and invite that flame to burn bright within us. This act is simplicity itself, and, just perhaps, after a lifetime of hardship and struggle, a few of us will achieve it and be set alight by it.

PART 1

THE WORD OF GOD

ONE
ONE

The Betrayer, the Betrayed, or the Beloved?

The betrayal of Judas, take 1

If there is any name that acts as a metonymy for betrayal then it is likely to be none other than that of Judas. The Christian tradition, which would appear to be in some way indebted to him for its very existence, is awash with images of the man as a demonic messenger, a lover of money, and a traitor to the Son of Man. For some, Judas is not simply an evil individual, seeking the satisfaction of his own insidious desires, but rather is portrayed as the very embodiment of evil on earth, a metaphysical manifestation of all that is opposed to the good, the noble, and the just. Thus the anathema of the Church against him is viewed as entirely justified; he not only betrayed innocent blood but also spilled the very blood of God. Judas did not conspire merely in a murder but in a deicide.

This popular view of Judas maintains the position that, regardless of what transpired from the act in question, the infamous betrayal was conceived and carried out by a criminal mind that was prepared to sacrifice the Messiah for a handful of silver coins. Regardless of how God employed that treacherous kiss, or how subsequent events redeemed it, the act itself is still to be condemned in the strongest possible manner.

Indeed, upon first reading the biblical narrative, one would deem this to be the only plausible account. While in the Gospel according to Mark, the earliest Gospel, we find no explicit explanation as to why Judas decided to betray Christ,[2] we read in Matthew that money is the principal cause.[3] The Gospel according to Luke, written at around the same time, mentions an additional reason, claiming that Satan had entered Judas, encouraging him to commit the act.[4] In John, the latest Gospel, we find that Judas seems primarily inspired by demonic influence.[5] Then, to top all this off, in the book of Acts, we discover a particularly gruesome end to the betrayer. Here we read that "with the reward he got for his wickedness, Judas bought a field; there he fell headlong, his body burst open and all his intestines spilled out." We go on to find that, according to this account, his death earned this plot of land the description "Field of Blood."[6]

The betrayal of Judas, take 2

However, when confronted with this traditional reading of the Judas/Jesus relationship, one must wonder who the real betrayer of the story is. For if, as an initial reading of the text would imply, the betrayal was deemed necessary for the rise of Christianity and the fulfillment of God's will, then we are presented with the image of Judas as one who was in fact central to the outworking of a divinely ordained plan.

With this in mind one might ask whether it was really Judas who was betrayed by Jesus rather than the other way around. Is it not true that Judas believed that he had been called to partake in the abundant life promised by Christ? Is it not likely that he believed he would find freedom, liberation, and purpose as a disciple of Jesus? Yet the traditional reading of the story would seem to suggest that Judas was really called to fulfill the role of an expendable pawn in a cosmic game.

The Gospel according to John portrays Jesus as knowing, at a very early stage, about what was going to take place.[7] In other words, he knew what would transpire from the very beginning, long before Judas would have ever even conceived of the plan. If this is true, if Jesus did know what Judas was capable of from early on, then the narrative compels us to ask why he called him to be a disciple in the first place. Or why Jesus did not endeavor to both warn him about his weakness for money and to ensure that he was never in a position to give in to such temptation. Surely, if someone knowingly offers a recovering alcoholic some wine, then that person is implicated in the consequences. The ultimate betrayal, according to this traditional reading, could thus be said to be the one perpetrated by Jesus against Judas, rather than the other way around. The ambiguity of the phase "the betrayal of Judas" captures this undecidability in the traditional reading beautifully: in the Gospels do we witness the betrayal of Judas (against Jesus) or the betrayal of Judas (by Jesus)?

The misguided fidelity of Judas

While there is a certain ambiguity within the traditional reading of the story regarding who the ultimate betrayer really was, Judas is still viewed as corrupt and evil (in the second reading his moral weakness is merely manipulated to fulfill a divine purpose). Yet there is another way of reflecting upon the actions of Judas, one that argues that it is very possible for Judas to have had less insidious motives for handing over his teacher, motives that were not so selfish after all. For instance, it is quite possible to imagine that Judas was actually attempting to force a confrontation between Jesus and the chief priests, a confrontation that would destroy the unjust power and authority of the latter. After all, it would seem that many, including the disciples, expected Jesus to directly confront the dominant religious and political powers of the day, setting in motion a revolution that would result in the establishment of an earthly Messianic kingdom. Indeed the title "Iscariot" hints at the possibility that Judas had once been a member of the zealots, a sect who advocated a violent revolution that would enshrine the rule of God within a political system.[8] With this in mind one could argue that Judas, frustrated by the lack of concrete political action among the disciples, was actually attempting to force Jesus' hand, placing him in a situation in which he would have to act in a decisive manner against the ruling powers.

It is not difficult for us to imagine this whenever we remind ourselves that Jesus had taught his disciples to confront those who they believed were in sin. By bringing Jesus face to face with the temple hierarchy, Judas perhaps hoped that Jesus' call for repentance, along with a demonstration of his power, would be enough to revolutionize the religious system. This interpretation is not without biblical support. For instance, it can help us to appreciate the description of Judas' death as found in the Gospel according to Matthew. In contrast to the description in the book of Acts, the Gospel of Matthew paints an image of Judas as one who, racked with guilt, gave the money back to the authorities before hanging himself. Because the money had been given in exchange for the betrayal of innocent blood, the religious authorities could not put it back into the temple treasury and so used it to buy a field, calling it the "Field of Blood" to signify that it had been bought with blood money.[9] Rather than Judas' stomach bursting open, as if by some divine act of retribution, we are presented with a broken man who experienced such deep regret for what had transpired that he committed suicide. It is difficult to interpret this as the act of a cold and remorseless killer who had carefully planned the arrest and execution of Jesus. Rather it seems to be more in line with the act of one who had set in motion a series of events with results that were both unforeseen and undesired.

The obedience of Judas

At this point we have considered the image of Judas first as a betrayer, second as betrayed, and third as misguided. There is however another possibility, one that may seem more shocking than any of these. For one may ask if there is a hint within the Gospels that Jesus not only knew that Judas would betray him, or willed this betrayal so as to fulfill a divine plan, but actually commanded Judas to betray him. We have already noted that the Gospel of John informs us that, at an early stage, Jesus knew what Judas was going to do. What if Jesus knew at an early stage precisely because Jesus was planning to ask him to do it?

If we pay close attention to the Gospel of Mark we find at least some hints that such an idea is plausible. In order to draw this out more explicitly we must consider what is said to take place moments before Judas approaches the chief priests and elders. Just before this infamous encounter between Judas and the temple authorities, we find that Jesus is in Bethany with his disciples at the home of Simon the Leper. While they are eating dinner a woman enters with an alabaster jar full of richly scented, expensive perfume. Without any encouragement she approaches Jesus and carefully breaks this jar above his head so that the perfume drips down over his entire body. Some of those present express anger at this excessive act, arguing that the perfume could have been sold and the money distributed among the poor (which, by the way, is exactly the type of response we ought to expect from those who had lived with Jesus). But surprisingly, Jesus responds to this remark by rebuking his friends, informing those gathered that the woman was acting in accordance with divine will because she was preparing his body for burial. Once Jesus has said this, Judas rises, leaves that place, and goes to the chief priests with his deal.[10]

The questions that immediately spring to mind when reading this narrative include (1) how did the woman know to engage in this symbolic act? (2) how did Jesus know what this act signified? and (3) why did this event seem to act as the catalyst for Judas' act of betrayal? A careful reading compels us to wonder whether some previous discussions had taken place, hidden from prying eyes. One wonders whether Jesus, Judas, and this mysterious woman had actually met together previously in a clandestine location so as to carefully script the upcoming events.

This scenario gains a small amount of credulity when we note (1) how Jesus comments that a betrayal must take place in order to fulfill the Scriptures;[11] (2) the way in which Jesus said to Judas, just after the infamous kiss, "*Friend,* do what you came for";[12] and (3) the fact that Jesus is presented as knowing in advance about the act, even asking that Judas perform it quickly.[13] In cinematic terms we find a powerful exploration of this interpretation in Martin Scorsese's *The Last Temptation of Christ* (1988). This adaptation from Nikos Kazantzakis's novel of the same name presents the relationship between Judas and Jesus as deep and loving. In the film both are presented as revolutionaries, but while Judas is dedicated to the violent overthrow of Roman rule, Jesus is seeking a revolution through the power of love. As the film unfolds, Jesus' ministry takes him to Jerusalem, where he finds the temple overrun by moneychangers. After overturning their tables he leads a small army against the temple rulers. Yet, at the last moment, he refuses to give in to the temptation of violence and, on the threshold of the temple, returns to his message of love. But this message also requires bloodshed, because for his revolution to take hold he must not kill but rather die, he must lead as a martyr rather than as a tyrant. If Jesus is ready to die then he must turn to one who he knows is ready to kill. And so he turns to Judas. In tears, Judas agrees.

One immediate problem with attempting to re-read the narrative in this way concerns the seeming anathema pronounced against Judas in the Gospel of Matthew in which Jesus says, "But woe to that man who betrays the Son of Man! It would be better for him if he had not been born."[14] Yet, on closer inspection, these words may yield a very different meaning to what we at first assume. For although these words are traditionally presumed to represent some kind of curse and condemnation, the wider biblical context mitigates against such a reading. First, why would Jesus curse the one who was about to betray him? Did Jesus himself not teach that one must bless those who seek to harm us? Second, such pronouncements of woe in ancient Judaism are generally expressions of love and concern rather than hatred or retribution.[15] And finally, did not Judas himself, as portrayed in the Gospel of Matthew, judge that it would have been better had he never been born—thus giving weight to the possibility that these words were said with heartfelt pain and foreknowledge rather than in a spirit of hatred and desire for revenge?[16]

Is it possible then that Jesus himself not only wanted Judas to betray him but actually demanded it? Is it possible that Jesus, as portrayed in the Gospel of Mark, possessed the insight that for his mission to expand and impact the whole world, this betrayal needed to take place? And is it then possible that this singular betrayal is one that actually testifies to a profound fidelity? It is with such a reading in mind that the philosopher and cultural theorist Slavoj Žižek goes so far as to write that, while "in all other religions, God demands that His followers remain faithful to Him—only Christ asked his followers to *betray* Him in order to fulfil His mission."[17]

It should be pointed out that this rather unorthodox re-imagining of the Judas/Jesus relationship, whether it has any basis in reality or not, is not an endorsement of the Gnostic figure that we encounter in the *Gospel of Judas,* a figure who gives up Jesus so as to free him from the confines of the mundane material world, the Judas to whom the Gnostic Jesus says, "For you will sacrifice the man that clothes me."[18] For, in stark contrast, the betrayal as presented in the canonical Gospels is one that brings about great mental and physical suffering to Jesus rather than an anticipation of freedom and liberation, so much so that the Gospel of Matthew informs us that, shortly before Judas approaches, Jesus tells his disciples, "My soul is overwhelmed with sorrow to the point of death."[19] More than this, the Gnostic interpretation is focused upon Jesus escaping from the material world, while the betrayal described above is precisely the means by which Jesus enters into the world in a more radical and universal way, becoming present at every place where the naked are clothed, the starving are fed, and the thirsty are given water.

What would Jesus do?

With all these possible readings is it any wonder that various poets, artists, and philosophers throughout the ages have been intrigued by the actions of Judas and unconvinced by the commonly accepted interpretation? The Gospels leave us with an ambiguous yet mesmerizing act, an act that has allowed poets and literary figures the freedom to pose interesting questions and lead us into reflections upon fascinating scenarios. Indeed the polymorphous nature of the text itself ensures that a single interpretation of Judas and his motives lies beyond the realm of biblical theology and finds its true home in the wide expanse of the artistic imagination.

Regardless of which account does the most justice to the events that took place all those years ago,[20] such discussion opens us up to conceive the difficulty of viewing this act as a simple and straightforward act of betrayal. The involvement of God, the complicity of Jesus, and the eventual outcome of the act all point to a situation that is far from simple to understand. Indeed, one begins to understand that a betrayal may be approached as an act of fidelity if looked at in a different light. In order to see this, let us take into consideration a recently discovered fragment from the long-lost *Gospel of Peter*.

Early that evening, while the other disciples were busy preparing for the upcoming Feast of Unleavened Bread,

Judas fell into a deep and unexpected sleep. As he lay there without moving he received a vision of the future. In this vision Judas saw himself with the other disciples as they shared a Passover meal with Jesus. During the meal he could hear his master speak solemnly about his own death while breaking bread and pouring wine. Then the vision progressed and Judas saw himself secretly meeting with the chief priests and agreeing to hand Jesus over to them. The vision continued by showing Judas kissing Jesus in the Garden of Gethsemane followed swiftly by the arrest, trial, torture, and death of Jesus. Yet the dream did not end there; instead, Judas went on to witness his own sorrow and remorse at his acts and to witness firsthand his own suicide. This was immediately followed by a deep pain as he was confronted with wave after wave of condemnations and judgment aimed at him through the ages. Yet in this vision he also witnessed the resurrection and ascension of Christ. He saw the spread of Jesus' message, its victory over the forces of Rome and the way in which it transformed the lives of countless millions. When Judas awoke from this dream he remembered some words that had been spoken to him by Jesus, "The hour has come for the Son of Man to be glorified. Very truly I tell you, unless a kernel of wheat falls to the ground and dies, it remains only a single seed. But if it dies, it produces many seeds. Those who love their life will lose it, while those who hate their life in this world will keep it for eternal life."[21]

In light of this startling new evidence let us imagine for a moment that we are the ones in this situation, awaking from this horrifying dream. In the aftermath of such a vision, the question we would have to ask is, "What would Jesus do?" For Judas to betray Jesus without any knowledge of what would transpire may well represent the ultimate act of betrayal, but here we must ask whether choosing these actions with foreknowledge would represent the ultimate act of fidelity.

Carrying the cross

There are countless people who betray Christianity, individuals who turn their backs on its message because they no longer believe in it or because it asks too much of them. But there are a few who betray Christianity, not because they no longer believe in it, but because they believe in it so deeply, because they understand that *unless the seed of our Christianity falls to the ground and dies it will remain a single seed, but if it is allowed to die it will produce many seeds.*

With this in mind we may wonder whether the deepest cost entailed in embracing the radical message of Christ—that we lay down our life and pick up our cross and follow him—may not simply be the call to sacrifice our own life (something we are asked to do *before* we pick up the cross), but the call to sacrifice what we love more than our life.

The cost of Christianity, for so many, is thought to lie in the demand that we die to ourselves for the sake of our

Christianity. The cross we are called to carry is thus one upon which we are to be put to death. But what if this cross we bear had another meaning? What if the cross that we are called to carry is not for us at all but rather, like the cross that Simon of Cyrene labored beneath, is really for another—a cross for us to crucify what we love? Is it possible that the cross we labor beneath must be used to crucify our Christianity? How many of us can truly understand this question? How many of us can really know what it is like to destroy what we love for the sake of what we love—to be the most faithful of betrayers? Yet perhaps it is precisely this that we are being called to: engaging in that most difficult task of putting our religion to death so that a religion without religion can spring forth.

TWO

Abraham as the Father of Faith(ful Betrayal)

Opposites attract

All this talk of crucifying Christianity must, I admit, seem rather impious to many ears. For surely our Christian faith is what we must accept at all costs, what we must courageously embrace, bow down before, and stand up to defend. Is this type of fidelity not the very virtue that we witness in the lives and deaths of martyrs throughout history? How is it possible to even contemplate Judas as someone whom Christians could or should consider a model of faith? The idea of Judas as a moral example would be laughable if it were not so distasteful. Judas is nothing less than a monster who can only be redeemed in the perverted minds of those who are seduced by the most ridiculous type of free-floating biblical revisionism. Christ would never ask that we betray our Christianity, for our Christianity is derived from the life and teachings of Christ. Surely then, if there is a human being whom we should model our lives upon it is Abraham, the famous father of faith, rather than Judas, the infamous betrayer of it.

The towering figure of Abraham overshadows the entire plain of the Judeo-Christian Scriptures. An initial reading of his momentous life shows that he stood opposed to everything that we traditionally associate with the figure of Judas. For while Judas is commonly understood as having let go of God for the sake of earthly treasure, Abraham let go of his earthly treasure, his own son, for the sake of God. While Judas is the ultimate betrayer, Abraham is the true father and figure of faith.

Yet perhaps Abraham and Judas, far from standing in utterly incommensurable opposition to each other—indwelling two different worlds, separated by two different testaments, and presenting two diametrically opposed responses to God—may actually have a more intimate relationship than we initially imagine.

Abraham and absolute fidelity

The perennial reason for which Abraham has been honored with the hallowed title "father of the faith" derives from his obedience to a terrifying call from God that asked him to murder his son as a sacrifice in the mountainous region of Moriah. The story informs us that, in response to this divine call, Abraham prepared transport and enough wood for the sacrificial fire before ascending a mountain chosen by God. Then, at a suitable place, he carefully constructed an altar with the wood, bound his son with rope, and placed him upon the mound. Without hesitation he then pulled out a knife and raised it high above his head. But at that moment, seconds before the knife was to plunge deep into the heart of his son, a voice from heaven cried out, "Abraham! Abraham!" and commanded that he lay down his weapon.[22]

In the now standard reading of this story, it is said that Abraham acted with absolute fidelity to the call of God, for despite his deep love for Isaac and his sense of correct ethical conduct he was prepared to murder his own son for the sake of the divine command. Abraham was prepared to follow the solemn dictate of God regardless of the consequences, suspending the ethical for the religious. Although Abraham loved his son and believed that he was to be the arch through which his descendents would enter the world, Abraham obeyed God and resolved in his heart to commit the murder. We must not in any way shy away from the fact that Abraham was a murderer, for at the very point when he decided to thrust that knife into the heart of his son, the radical act of renunciation had occurred and the transgression against both his son and the natural law— that one ought to protect the life of the innocent—had been committed.

One of the standard Christian interpretations of this story involves drawing out the similarity that exists between this test and the idea that Jesus was sacrificed by God on our behalf. But is not another analogy possible, not one between Abraham and God but rather between Abraham and the betrayer of God?

Upon reading the stories of Abraham and Judas, we are confronted with the fact that both individuals are divinely chosen for a murderous task: they are both required to sacrifice one to whom they are intimately related, and both renounce their victim. One pertinent difference is of course that Abraham receives Isaac back, while Judas fails to receive Jesus back. But surely this is because Judas commits suicide before such an encounter can take place. The Gospel narratives present us with the idea that a reencounter and possible reconciliation between Jesus and Judas would have happened had he not taken his own life.

The two stories are so similar that we can imagine the creation of a possible novel related to the Passion in which Jesus convinces Judas to commit the betrayal by relating the story of Abraham and Isaac. In this novel we could imagine a scene in which Judas goes on to kill himself in utter despair, wondering why he had not received Jesus back from the dead. We can imagine reading of Judas watching in disbelief as Jesus is crucified, weeping as he recalls the promise Jesus had made to him that, just as Abraham received Isaac back, so, if he had faith, he would receive his Lord back. In this story it would be presented as if it was only after the crucifixion of Jesus that Judas truly loses faith rather than before it. Here we would read of Judas as a type of failed Abraham, although who knows what Abraham would have done had the knife plunged into the heart of his beloved son and he was required to wait.

It is not then the acts of Abraham and Judas that are fundamentally distinct but rather the difference between how they are perceived. The difference between them comes down to the way their motives are understood. For both involve the sacrifice of another and both involve acting in response to a higher will.[23]

Wrestling with God

B y beginning with a reflection upon Judas (the betrayer) followed by Abraham (the father of faith) we can begin to see that an act that may appear to be a betrayal of faith (that of Judas) could be an act of deep fidelity to it (that of Abraham).

The relationship between fidelity and betrayal in the Judeo-Christian tradition is further complicated in the Scriptures via stories that seem to suggest that one must wrestle with, disagree with, and even disobey God for the sake of retaining one's fidelity to God. Let us look at three different examples.

First, let us remain a little longer with Abraham. Before we ever reach the story of his being called to sacrifice his son, it is significant to note that we come across a very interesting situation in which Abraham seems to directly question the actions of God in the face of what would seem to be divine injustice. Thus we find that Abraham is not some weak-willed individual afraid to question what he believes to be wrong. In Genesis 18 we read that God is openly contemplating whether or not to destroy the city of Sodom because of its excessive immorality. In the story God is, at first, merely interested in finding out whether the quantity of sinful activity within the city is sufficiently high to justify its total destruction.[24] However, Abraham responds to hearing this with a question that causes God to reconsider. Abraham plucks up his courage and asks whether God would really be justified in destroying the city if there were fifty righteous people within its walls, regardless of the quantity of sin. In response, God seems persuaded and agrees. Yet Abraham does not stop there, for now that he has been able to shift God's perspective and consider the individuals who dwell in the city, he decides to push further and ask whether God would really be justified in destroying the city if there were forty-five righteous people. Again God agrees that it would be better to let Sodom remain if there were forty-five righteous people housed within its walls. This discussion continues until Abraham has persuaded God to hold back from destroying the city so long as there are as few as ten righteous people living there. Regardless of how one wishes to interpret the nature of this dialogue, it is obvious that the narrative affirms (1) that Abraham felt able to question God and (2) that God did not seem to mind being questioned. The story even seems to imply that God wants Abraham to disagree, for why else would God be presented as openly and audibly considering whether or not to destroy Sodom within earshot of Abraham?

The second example goes a little further than the last one and relates to the biblical figure Jacob. One night when Jacob was camped out near the ford of Jabbok we read that a stranger approached and started a fight with Jacob that lasted all through the night. The stranger in question is said to have been unable to overpower Jacob and so demanded that he be set free from Jacob's grip. But Jacob refused, demanding that the stranger bless him before he would let him go. In response the stranger said, "Your name will no longer be Jacob, but Israel, because you have struggled with God and with human beings and have overcome."[25]

Whereas Abraham questioned God with a certain deference and respect, this story presents Jacob in a much more defiant and aggressive light. Jacob does not seem in any way repentant when he discovers who this stranger really is, and God, far from seeming to have a problem with such an unrepentant follower, bestows the victor with the blessing of a new name that would come to represent, not only Jacob, but all of his descendants.

It is here, in this encounter between Jacob and God, that we discover why the Jewish community is marked out by the name "Israel." This title represents the spirit of a people who have "wrestled with God and with men and have overcome." This name illuminates the living dynamic of Hebraic faith. It magnifies a radical idea that marks out the Jewish people, describing something almost paradoxical about this faith: that absolute commitment to God involves a deep and sustained wrestling with God. In this story we discover that the Israelites are to be marked out, not as a people who live out their faith through unquestioning submission but as a people who demonstrate their love and commitment to the source of their faith in a radical commitment to fighting with that source. This is a people to be marked out by struggling, by passion, by critical engagement.

The name *Israel* is not some kind of curse, or dispassionate description, it is a blessing. Here God does not merely describe something that the Israelites do; the name describes what they ought to be. The people of God do not merely adopt this name; they are inscribed within it and they affirm it in the fabric of their lives. While the Islamic faith is derived from a word that can be translated as "submission," the tribes of Israel bear a different name, one that evokes the image of conflict, tension, and turmoil. Thus, if relationship with God within this tradition is to be understood as promising peace and harmony, it cannot be understood as a peace and harmony that stands in contrast to a kinetic life of tension, striving, and conflict. For the blessing that God bestowed upon Jacob brings us face to face with the fact that God wants a fight.

For a New Testament example of this wrestling let us briefly note an interesting event to be found in the book of Acts. In Acts 10 we are told that Peter falls into a trance and experiences a vision in which he is informed that he can eat animals that were previously considered unclean within the Jewish religious system. Here we read,

> About noon the following day as they were on their journey and approaching the city, Peter went up on the roof to pray. He became hungry and wanted something to eat, and while the meal was being prepared, he fell into a trance. He saw heaven opened and something like a large sheet being let down to earth by its four corners. It contained all kinds of four-footed animals, as well as reptiles and birds. Then a voice told him, "Get up, Peter. Kill and eat."

"Surely not, Lord!" Peter replied. "I have never eaten anything impure or unclean."

The voice spoke to him a second time, "Do not call anything impure that God has made clean."

This happened three times, and immediately the sheet was taken back to heaven.[26]

This vision fundamentally challenges what Peter holds to be the command of God and opens up a difficult dilemma: in order to obey the command of God he must disobey the command of God.

The serpent versus God

The interesting feature about the above examples is that each of them brings the reader face to face with a time when individuals have questioned, fought, and even betrayed the word of God as a direct result of their fidelity to the way of God. More than this, each of these examples is framed in such a way that the reader is left in no doubt that the wrestling was acceptable to, and even desired by, God. Yet the text is structured in such a way that it challenges us to go deeper, for it does not merely offer us examples of people who wrestled with God but also presents us with situations in which we are invited to do the same. The text itself places us into various situations where the God we read about is one whom we must question, not out of our weakness and selfishness but rather from out of the very depths of our faith.

One of the clearest examples of this relates to the first great conflict described within the Bible, the conflict between God, the first humans, and a cunning serpent. Contrary to what we may have been told, this event is not depicted as a great battle between God and the devil, for regardless of the serpent's motives, it is never described as Satan. In fact the serpent's motives, upon closer reading, appear rather ambiguous. Indeed there is a wonderful Jewish mythology that claims to reveal the true identity of the serpent, an identity that turns out to be rather surprising. (In chapter four we will reveal this identity.)

The story itself informs us that in the beginning God formed a tree in the center of Eden and named it "the tree of the knowledge of good and evil." Adam and Eve were forbidden to eat of its fruit with the warning that, if they consumed its fruit, they would surely die. The truth that God did not reveal was that, if one ate from the tree, one would immediately gain knowledge of good and evil and become like God. Into this scenario enters a snake with an unnerving ability to talk. This snake addresses Eve and encourages her to question God's prohibition, telling her truthfully that she will not die upon eating the fruit. Indeed the snake also reveals to her what God had concealed, namely that this fruit would bestow deep insight into the nature of good and evil and enable them to become like the divine.

With such an appealing possibility laid before them, it is not long before both Eve and Adam pick some fruit from the tree and begin to eat of it. When God eventually finds out what has happened, God becomes angry and curses them.

To the serpent God declares that both it and its descendants will crawl upon their belly for the duration of their existence. Then, between male and female, God places enmity and discord. To women God also declares that childbirth will be painful and that they will be subject to the rule of men. To men God pronounces a curse on the ground upon which they labor so that they will always have to struggle for food. We are then introduced to another tree in the garden called the "tree of life," a tree with fruit that bestows everlasting life to those who eat of it. So that Adam and Eve will not become immortal, God banishes them from Eden and places both cherubim and a flaming sword at the entrance to prevent them from re-entering.[27]

From Sunday school to the church pulpit, from religious tracts to devotional books, this story has been presented as a basic tale detailing how human beings, from time immemorial, selfishly chose to disobey their loving God. Yet a close and faithful reading reveals a much more controversial possibility, for this story itself presents us with a deep level of ambiguity, a disconcerting moral dilemma, and a cosmic twist that makes Dan Brown's latest religious ponderings seem rather unimaginative. Indeed, it is amazing that any preacher would want to go near this subversive narrative or any churchgoing parent would want to share it with their child. For if we attempt to follow the grain of the story we are forced to reassess whom we consider to be just and whom we consider to be unjust. While it initially seems obvious that we ought to side with God against the serpent's act of sedition, the story itself causes us to question such an assumption.

To be a biblical literalist means that one attempts to attend to the text as it stands before us rather than importing foreign ideas, regardless of how obvious they may seem. In this way I wish to steadfastly affirm biblical literalism; I wish to stand side by side with the Christian fundamentalist who demands that we let the text speak for itself. Of course I also wish to be informed by the scholars who engage in biblical criticism. But this does not in any way stand opposed to the attempt to attend to the text as we have received it in its final form. And so, as a literalist of sorts, I must chide any so-called literalist who would secretly import foreign Greek philosophy into this narrative by assuming that God must, of necessity, be right and the serpent wrong.[28] There is little evidence of this reading within the story itself, if we want to read it literally, that is.

Coming to the story as it stands, it is difficult to unquestionably side with God. Upon reading the story, one is confronted with a variety of problems. For instance, why is it wrong to want to be like God, knowing the difference between good and evil? Is it not the case that some of the greatest saints we have ever known have spent their entire lives attempting to be like God in both their mind and actions, going so far as calling this pursuit the highest good? Also, even if eating of this fruit were a cosmic criminal act, it is difficult to see how the punishment is in any way commensurate to the crime.

In short, the story possesses a deep and fascinating ambiguity, so much so that it helped to fuel a third-century Gnostic sect called the Ophites (*Ophis* meaning snake), who

actually sided with the snake in the whole Genesis affair.
It is difficult to say much about this little group, as what
we know about them is derived almost exclusively from the
writings of those who opposed them. However we do know
that they understood the snake of Genesis to be a type of
Promethean hero who stood up against the God-tyrant in
an attempt to set humans free. We can see a glimpse of this
when we consider what Hippolytus wrote about them.

> This serpent is the strength that stood by Moses,
> and the staff that turned into a snake. . . . This all-
> comprehending serpent is the wise logos of Eve. That is
> the mystery of Eden, the sign over Cain, that no one who
> found him might kill him. The serpent is Cain, whose
> sacrifice was not accepted by the God of this world: he
> accepted the bloody sacrifice of Abel instead, for the
> Lord of this world is well pleased with blood. And it
> is the serpent that in latter days, at the time of Herod,
> appeared in the form of a man. . . . So none can be saved
> and rise again without the Son, who is the serpent. His
> image was the bronze serpent held up by Moses in the
> desert. That is the meaning of the words (John 3:14):
> "And as Moses lifted up the serpent in the wilderness,
> so must the Son of Man be lifted up."[29]

The Ophites sought to add scriptural weight to their sect
by relating the curse given to the serpent by God in Genesis
to the death of Christ on the Cross, arguing that both
suffered at the hands of the divine for attempting to open

the eyes of the people. They advocated a type of religious anarchy directed against God, an anarchy that they believed was birthed from the biblical text itself.

It would be a mistake to think that such Gnostic ideas were rejected by the church authorities because they stood in such direct opposition to the Bible and were therefore implausible (for, if this were the case, then their falsity would be evident to all). Rather, the problem for the church lay precisely in the opposite problem: such a view of God seemed deeply plausible and thus required a rigorous rebuttal. My point here is not to make the claim that these antagonisms and ambiguities in Genesis point toward the existence of a Gnostic subterranean narrative nestled deep within the Scriptures, one that presents God as a tyrant who must be resisted at all costs. My point is rather to show how such a view gained plausibility because the story itself is infused with ambiguities.

It is also worth noting that this is not the only example of the text placing us into the rather awkward position of needing to wrestle with and question its descriptions of God. We are presented throughout with images of the divine that are morally questionable. For instance, we must wrestle with the idea of the God of peace and forgiveness acting as a heartless warrior who endorses the Israelite massacre of three thousand Levites and the population of Canaan. We are driven to question the image of an all-loving God as nationalistic, as advocating the theft of land and of endorsing the ownership of slaves. And we must struggle with the idea that this God of liberation is slow to be moved by injustice, for instance, when the Israelites are enslaved by the Egyptians.

And so, even with the few examples we have looked at above, it would seem almost impossible to argue that the biblical narrative is a calm, clear, and uncontentious text. Rather, the Scriptures reach our ears in an often ominous and scandalous tone. From the opening pages of this ancient text, we are confronted with a shocking series of ambiguous stories and complex conflicts that defy easy categorization and interpretation.[30]

When faced with these conflicts there are two common responses. One involves attempting to explain them away in an attempt to defend the idea that the text is the divine Word and that the idea of God we find there is in fact coherent. The other involves affirming the conflicts and rejecting the idea that this text is divine. While one seeks to maintain the divine status of the book through calming the conflicts and reconciling the differences, the other rejects this divine status by arguing that the text cannot be rendered coherent without the most outlandish interpretive gymnastics. But what if we are not forced to choose between these two positions? What if we can affirm these conflicts at one and the same moment that we affirm the idea of this text being deeply branded by the white-hot presence of God? Indeed, what if the conflict we encounter in the examples above is precisely what we would expect to find in a text claiming divine status rather than something that witnesses against it?

THREE

THREE

The Biblical "wHole"

Divine antagonism

In the last chapter we began to look at how parts of the Judeo-Christian narrative are marked by a wrestling with God. We noted further how the reader is regularly confronted with rather chaotic and contradictory expressions of God that are often in conflict both with our own expectations and with the wider biblical context. The result of all this is an unnerving sense that biblical narrative is marked by a series of fissures and conflicts that render it fractured, fragmented, and incomplete. It would seem then that any attempt to ever sketch out a single grand cartography of the text would be doomed to failure.

In recognition of this, many claim that these tensions and conflictory claims count against the idea that this work is anything other than a human creation. It is argued that such tensions are exactly what we would expect to find from a purely human construction pieced together over such a wide expanse of time. The argument is often made that once we recognize that a literal reading of the Bible throws up a multitude of fractures, ruptures, and antagonisms, then we can no longer testify to its divine status. To take the Bible literally would involve recognizing the wounded nature of the words and, as such, rejecting them.

In one important respect this idea of rejecting the Bible because of internal fractures and tensions is in profound agreement with what many church authorities proclaim, namely that if the text is at war with itself then it cannot possibly be the Word of God. Thus, for so much of the Church, there is a desire to demonstrate that there is no antagonism or contradiction within the Bible, that its message is analogous to a magnificent orchestral piece in which all the parts move in perfect harmony with each other.

But what both these perspectives fail to acknowledge is the possibility that we are not actually caught on the horns of a dilemma in which we must either reject the various antagonisms so as to maintain the claim that the text is divinely inspired, or accept the antagonisms and thus reject it. For, if we shift our focus, it is possible to see that these ripples and ruptures within the text, far from counting against the work as something divinely inspired, are exactly what we would expect to find from that which is marked by and born out of the very depths of God.

Modern inerrancy

By mentioning these antagonisms I want to avoid getting caught up in the debates that take place within biblical criticism. These debates relate to issues such as how editors have forged certain parts of the Bible from a variety of older sources and explorations into the various ideological clashes being played out within the pages of the text. These are interesting questions to explore and draw us into the world of formal biblical studies as well as the modernistic claims of those who affirm biblical inerrancy. It is worth noting that both biblical criticism and apologists for the idea of inerrancy are primarily concerned with the rational legitimacy of the text when viewed as a description of factual claims. While biblical criticism examines these claims without presupposing that the words are divinely given, the approach of the modern inerrancy writers is one that affirms the absolute factual accuracy of the text and then seeks to explain away any conflicts. While these two approaches may seem diametrically opposed, those who advocate the inerrancy of Scriptures today have actually been profoundly influenced by the thinking that gave birth to the modern, critical disciplines. While those who advocate biblical inerrancy reject many of the findings of historical criticism, they still attempt to justify their own claims via the rational approach that historical criticism also employs. In doing so the fundamentalist is claiming that the truth of the Bible is tied up with factual claims that can be intellectually defended. As such, those institutions that advocate biblical inerrancy expend a great deal of time and energy attempting to offer explanations that will effectively reconcile any problems that they are presented with in the Bible. Yet it is this very process of rational justification that makes fundamentalism a very modern phenomenon, one that sets it at odds with the more ancient tradition of inerrancy found within the Church.

Medieval theologians such as Peter Damien would have rejected these modern attempts to explain any tensions and conflicts in the Bible through the use of reason, judging that such a procedure would involve raising human reason above the acts of God. While it may seem somewhat strange to us today, if someone had pointed out to Damien that the Gospel of Luke places the Ascension of Jesus on the day of the Resurrection while the book of Acts tells us that it took place forty days after the Resurrection, he would likely have simply accepted both readings without attempting to explain the discrepancy the way in which modern inerrantists would. He would probably be very happy to assert that God ascended into heaven on the date spoken of in Luke *and* the date spoken of in Acts while pointing out in no uncertain terms that Jesus ascended only once. As we can see, this type of approach is very different from that of the modern inerrancy movement, a movement that seeks to provide a rational account for the differences. Thus, from this perspective, the supposedly uncompromising stance of fundamentalism could be said to involve far too much compromise.

If I am taking sides with anyone at this point it is with the pre-modern inerrancy approach, at least in one important respect. While I am an advocate of biblical criticism, I wish to argue that a truly religious reading of the text involves bracketing out these questions and engaging with the text as it is received, without justifications or explanations. This does not mean that we have to place our critical faculties to one side when reading the Bible, somehow ignoring the various antagonisms at work there. It simply means that when engaging with it in the religious register, we bracket out such questions in order to perceive a spectral presence that lies beneath the various antagonisms that mark the text.

In this way one can say that an academic reading and a religious reading of the Bible do not clash in any way, for they operate in different, incommensurable registers and approach different dimensions of the text. For instance, when reading in Revelation about the 1,500 square mile New Jerusalem descending from heaven, with walls of jasper and streets constructed from pure gold, the religious reader does not ask whether or not something like this is possible but rather allows the image to burn itself into the imagination. The religious reader endeavors to approach the impenetrable source that gave birth to this wondrous image while simultaneously allowing the vision of an awe-inspiring city with gates that never shut, bathed in eternal light, overflowing with mercy and full of people from all nations to impact the way that we live today.

Second naïveté

This religious approach is not concerned with blindly accepting the claims of the text any more than it is concerned with rejecting them. Rather, it is solidly directed at the task of connecting with the primordial source of the text in all its terrifying and transformative dimensions.

Philosophically speaking, such an approach to the text can be said to involve a type of second naïveté. Whenever we first come to the text as religious readers, we all too often approach it in a naïve manner that interprets the various scientific, geographical, historical, and metaphysical claims as constituting the truth of the text. Then, as these claims become increasingly difficult to hold uncritically, we often enter into a stage in which we question such assumptions and become interested in the various academic debates. However, it would be a mistake to think that this is the last word, for it is possible to take a further step by re-engaging with a naïve reading, but one that does not turn its back on critical thinking. Instead, this return to naïveté allows the individual temporarily to suspend such academic debates so as to open up a deeper mode of engagement with the text itself.

The point of second naïveté is not to reach a position where one rejects academic debates but rather to provide a space in which readers can place these ongoing debates to one side so that they can attend to the transforming source of the text itself. It is this transforming source that we speak of when we speak of the Word of God.

The devotional reader who enters into the space of second naïveté does not stop to wonder if, for example, the story of the prodigal son is based on an actual family or is a metaphor. Such readers do not attempt to pull out a series of propositional claims from the story or treat it as a scientific description. For the Word, if it exists at all, does not simply dwell in the ink that marks the pages of the Bible and cannot be isolated in a dissection of the story into its constituent parts. A devotional reading of the story considers it to be an overflowing container of life-giving meaning and, as such, engages in an imaginative interaction with it. Such a reading involves placing oneself into the narrative, inhabiting the different characters, dialoguing with them, filling in the gaps of the story with one's own experiences and ideas (which in the Jewish tradition is represented in the tradition of the Midrash). Here the Word is approached, not by focusing on the individual words but rather on the individual's imaginative, transformative interaction with the words and with the Event that gave birth to them.

The act of second naïveté is directly encouraged by the fact that there are various, often conflicting, accounts of God and faith at work in the Scriptures. The writers and redactors were happy to play with different images and metaphors that clashed. The sheer amount of ideological conflicts playing out within the text hints at the fact that the writers were writing about a reality that could not be reduced to one description, a reality that was testified to better in the clash of perspectives than in the development of a single, finely honed one. The text was written not to be approached as an academic document detailing facts about the life of faith but rather as an invitation into the life of faith. Hence, if we lose ourselves in a sea of discussions concerning the conflicts themselves we will fail to attend to the reality that the writers hint at as lying behind, beneath, and within the conflicts: the one we call God.

This diversity of views concerning God within the Scriptures is not the only thing that points to the ineffability of God. Not only do we find that God is presented in a variety of names, but also there are times when God is directly referred to as one who dwells beyond all names. For instance, the Tetragrammaton (a Greek term that means "the four letters") refers to the unspeakable four-letter name of God that is employed at various times within the Hebrew Bible. It is a word that lacks vowels and so cannot be said. In this way it acts as a reminder that God is a great mystery who lies beyond or before description. Later we shall also look at the encounter between Moses and God in the Midian desert as another example of this. But for now it is simply worth noting that the multitude of descriptions detailing the nature of God, combined with the various claims that God cannot be contained by any description, presents the reader with the reality that the text affirms God as beyond all our understandings of God. In other words, the God who grasps us is never grasped (in text, thinking, or experience).

These fractures, fissures, and impenetrable descriptions within the text point to the volcanic activity of an unspeakable Event at work there, an Event that is never directly revealed but rather is indirectly hinted at via the various narratives of liberation, freedom, homecoming, resurrection, salvation, peace, and rebirth that have been generated in the aftermath of an encounter with this source, themes that span the entire work. This unspeakable Event is thus affirmed by the narrative, housed within it, emanates from it, and yet is not of it.

The biblical parallax

To approach the Bible as indirectly drawing us toward an impenetrable source within and yet not contained by the words is to acknowledge its profoundly parallactical structure. At its most basic, the word *parallax* refers to the apparent shift of an object against its background due to a shift in the viewer's position. However, in philosophical terms a parallax shift takes on a more significant meaning that stretches beyond the rather mundane insight that an object will appear to be different when viewed from an alternative angle. Rather, in the more radical sense, to speak of a parallactical view is to refer to the phenomenon whereby a single object appears to change in a way that is *fundamentally opposed* to its previous manifestation simply because of the observer's change in position. A prime example of this in science would concern the composition of light. When viewed in one way light appears as a series of waves, but when viewed in a different way it appears to be composed of particles.

In the examples mentioned above, we can discern a parallactical structure within the biblical narrative itself analogous to that which we find in descriptions of light within physics or in the mind/brain debates that take place within psychology. In the same way that light seems to contain an impenetrable core that defies direct observation (being rendered as wave or particle depending upon the way one looks at it), so too when believers seek out an understanding of God they are left with different, often mutually exclusive, manifestations. The Bible testifies to this parallactical situation precisely in its rich cacophony of stories, parables, and teachings, all of which, when taken together, defy any vain attempt at rendering the source of faith into a simple, coherent vision.[31] The "true" description of God seems to lie always just beyond the reach of our grasp. The final "word" is always frustratingly elusive, dwelling just beyond the horizon of our thought, and the conflicting images that we encounter within the Bible continually remind us that the source of this living work is not captured in our petty observations. In acknowledging this, the believer testifies to the Scriptures as infused with a presence that dwells both in the midst and in excess of the text, a some(no)thing that cannot be contained within the narrative but that makes its presence felt in the fractures and ruptures within it. The words of the text, like Christ, are wounded.

From the void without to the void within

This idea of a rupture in the text that hints at the elusive presence of a divine Word is connected to the idea of eschatology within Christianity. *Eschatology* is a theological term that is often used within Christianity to refer to events that are to come. Christianity is thus thought to have an eschatological dimension insomuch as it looks forward to a kingdom that is not yet here, a beautiful realm of love, forgiveness, and mercy that we yearn for, long for, pray for, and prepare for. Here the eschatological kingdom of God is located in the not-yet of the future. However, within the

Bible we find a much more radical view of the eschatological kingdom, not as the absence of something that is to come, but rather as the absence of a kingdom that is already here. Indeed, this distinction is one of the prime differences between the message of John the Baptist and the message of Jesus. While John the Baptist preached that the kingdom was coming, Jesus preached that this kingdom was already among us.[32] However, in saying this he did not overturn the message of John the Baptist but rather deepened it, for Jesus spoke of a kingdom that was here and yet as simultaneously being something that was looked to as still to come.

Following the image of the kingdom that was spoken of by Jesus, we encounter the idea that while it is still thought of as "to come" this does not mean that it will one day arrive at the end of a certain period of time, but rather that the kingdom *is* "to come," that is, the kingdom is already among us but in a spectral manner that resists our grasp. Here the opening created by the eschatological kingdom of God is not an opening into the future but rather an opening into the present that acts much like the portable holes we see in cartoons that can be placed onto any solid surface, thus creating a gap. This view of the kingdom is something that we also find confirmed in the writings of Paul, such as when he speaks of the kingdom as both the now and the not-yet.[33]

Is this initially bizarre logic not what we also find being played out when we contemplate the presence of those whom we love? Is it not a great romantic truth that the presence of our beloved is always of a spectral kind? To truly know and love someone involves acknowledging that person's inscrutable eschatological depths, understanding that the presence of the one before us is always manifested as a type of absence, as an opening. For each person is a universe for us to explore. In this way it is wrong to imagine that we long for someone we love to enter into our world, to come. Rather, when the one we love arrives in our world we encounter that person as precisely the one who is "to come."

This is why our desire for those we love is born in our encounter with them rather than satisfied there. We cannot desire the one whom we do not know, for the simple reason that we do not know that person. We can only desire the one who is before us, the one who remains mysterious in his or her presence. The other is both the origin and the unreachable destination of our desire, for there is always something Other about the other, something "to come" amidst the presence of those we love. In the eyes of the beloved, a universe opens up and envelops us.

We find an interesting example of this structure in the long-running science fiction series *Doctor Who*. The Time Lord's Tardis (the vehicle he uses in order to travel through time and space) is radically smaller on the outside than it is on the inside. Indeed, while the exterior dimensions of the vehicle are the same as a mere telephone box, the interior is composed of a vast and seemingly unlimited expanse. In the same way, the small physical frame of our beloved belies the fact that it houses an interior world of seemingly unlimited proportions.

If we find this logic in the language of romanticism, that speaks of our beloved as the one who is encountered as still to come, then the idea may be expressed in philosophical terms as well. The idea that we encounter an inexpressible mystery within the world, rather than locating it somewhere outside the world, was developed by Georg Wilhelm Friedrich Hegel. For Immanuel Kant we must postulate the existence of a mysterious, otherworldly realm that he called the "numenal," a world that we cannot directly access but which we can dimly perceive as stretching beyond the world as we know it. Here our knowledge of the world is seen to include the recognition that our knowledge is limited to the purely phenomenal world. In other words, our thinking leads us to acknowledge that there is a realm that exists beyond all thought. For Hegel, however, this mystery was not something that lay beyond the world but rather penetrated it: the mystery was not "out there" but rather had set its tent up among us. Such an idea resonates to some extent with the words of Jesus when some Pharisees asked him when the kingdom would come. In response Jesus replied, "The coming of the kingdom of God is not something that can be observed, nor will people say, 'Here it is,' or 'There it is,' because the kingdom of God is in your midst."[34]

These romantic and philosophical descriptions are fundamentally seen at work in the biblical description of the Incarnation, where Jesus is described as the site in which God, as the Wholly Other, is no longer located "out there" but rather is inscribed in human flesh. In theological terms, God is neither reduced to human flesh, nor dwells outside the flesh, but rather is in, but not of, it. The mystery of God is not dissipated in Christ but brought near. Is this not the key to understanding the idea of transcendence within Christianity, a term that describes a way of breaking the here/elsewhere dichotomy of near and far through the idea of an immanence so deep and impenetrable that it cannot be approached? The mystery of God now dwells among us rather than standing above us.

In Christ, the absolute Other of God is said to enter into the mundane world and set up a home among us. Here God is neither reduced to the world of objects nor remains in some space utterly beyond the world, but rather ruptures the present with the future, fractures the finite with the infinite, and tears through the temporal with the eternal, inhabiting the now in the guise of the not-yet. Here God's Otherness is no longer located in some eschatological realm beyond the present order of the world but rather in an eschatological realm that infuses the present world, rupturing it and placing it into question. Here the razor-sharp cut of God's kingdom does not presuppose a hairline gap between the present world and the world to come, but rather is that which slices through the present world with the world to come, inhabiting our world with a divine realm that is not reducible to our time and space.

The point of all this is to acknowledge that one cannot gain a full picture of the biblical text, not because of the rather mundane insight that we will never be able to learn everything we need to know about history, geography, and so on, to gain a full insight into its true meaning, but rather because the text itself is rent by an interior eschatological void that can never be rendered whole and accessible to us.

In this way a certain form of tension, conflict, and rupture is present in the Word or, more accurately, the "Word" is hinted at in the tension, conflict, and rupture that we encounter in the words.

The biblical wHole

This deep eschatological wound within the text must not be confused with the Word of God but rather is a hint of this Word's occurrence, much as a crater is the sign that a volcano once erupted there. The Word itself, as we shall explore in section three, can be described as the Event that forms the crater. Here we can begin to perceive the idea of the Word of God as the happening of an unprecedented, volcanic activity. This activity is hinted at in the dynamic interweaving of the words expressed in the Bible, giving birth to those words, testifying to them but ultimately transcending them. This activity or event springs forth from a deep inner cavern that no words can claim access to. In this way the Word of God refers to what the believer encounters as a presence exploding from the heart of the text, a presence that can never be captured in some confession of faith or creedal formation, no matter how beautiful or profound it may be. Its energy cannot be reduced to some liturgical chant or rendered into a three-point presentation. The Word, if it exists at all, if "existence" is even the right word to describe its mode of dwelling, is not then the patch of meaning that covers over the wound of our unknowing but rather is that which causes the wound itself. The result

of this divine wound is sadly hinted at in the formation of
vast industries set up by those who would eagerly carve out
a living by providing religious patches. To truly approach
this Word is to be confronted with the rupture of Revelation
(a topic we will explore in section three).

At this point we simply need to note how, in so much of
the Church in the West today, there is an attempt at closing
over this traumatic rent in the text in one of two ways:

(1) By attempting to do away with the central antagonism,
    affirming one narrative expression over the others.

(2) By endeavoring to cover up the antagonism by attempting
    to create a master interpretation derived from molding
    together the various available interpretations.

In opposition to these attempts at closing over the
unspeakable rupture, a truly devotional reading of the text
involves encouraging this mystery to be made manifest *as*
a mystery and exploring how we are to celebrate, affirm,
invite, and recall that mystery. The theologian here acts
as a type of anti-theologian, for instead of placing God
(*theos*) into language (*logos*), the theologian can help us
to dive into the deep abyss of that mystery and cherish its
transformative power.

The idea of the "Word of God" becomes pale and anemic
when reduced to the idea of a factual description of historical
events. The words of the Bible, wonderful as they often are,
must not be allowed to stand in for God's majestic Word,
as if the words and phrases have been conferred with some
sacred status and the phonetic patterns given divine power.
Rather, the Word of God can be described as that dark core

around which the words of the text find their orbit, the unspeakable Source within the text that cannot be reduced to the words themselves but that breathes life into them.

The claim that the Bible is the Word of God, whether true or not, makes sense only if it refers to the source of the gaps between the words; or more precisely, the source of the irreducible Gap within the words themselves. God's Word is thus testified to indirectly by the parallactical nature of the text itself, being communicated by the rich, weaving web of wounded words that testify to the happening of a divine event.

So then, if we were to imagine someone rewriting the text in such a way that all the tensions and conflicts were exiled, if we were to do the impossible and render the text into the ultimate fantasy of the fundamentalist (a text at one with itself), then the Word of God would not be clearer; rather, the Word of God would have been systematically eradicated. This attempt to systematize the text would be nothing less than a form of exorcism in which the Word of God is cast out—removing the spirit until we are left with nothing but the letter of the law.

However, in response to those who would claim that the text is whole, we must not fall into the trap of merely affirming the opposite, of saying that the text is partial, incomplete, and multiple. Rather we must show how the text itself testifies to incompleteness within the complete and a multiplicity within the one. The eschatological must be shown to dwell within the text rather than merely outside it. The properly theological stance here is evidenced then in the attempt to take a view that acknowledges the dark core of Revelation testified to in the gap within the story: the traumatic core of a Revelation worthy of the capital "R." Here the text can be described neither as whole nor as partial but rather as *wHole*.

Indirectly approaching the Word

As most of us know, the Bible is often approached as a text that lays bare the mind of God, as that which graciously offers us a God's-eye view of the world. This view supposes that by reading the book faithfully we can uncover the intentions, ideas, and desires of the Creator. In contrast to this, I am charting the idea that we ought to approach the text as actually manifesting the felt concealment of God. Here the central Word of the text is never directly grasped as a source of knowledge, but rather is encountered as a life-transforming event.

The point then is not to engage in a hermeneutical approach that would seek to somehow expose the mind of God, but rather to embrace a radical hermeneutics (a reading that sets the text free from the idea of a single correct meaning) that seeks to ultimately move beyond the desire to reduce the text to descriptive statements, inviting instead an ongoing transformative dialogue with the text. This way of reading the Bible asks much more of each individual reader, and offers the professional Bible critic much less authority. For the idea of the Word of God as a description of the central Event that dwells within the words and yet is not of them (just as Jesus was in the world but not of it) helps us to understand that however interesting the work of the biblical scholars, the theologians, the fundamentalists, or the intellectual skeptics may be, the true depth of the text is not to be discovered by following their exacting methods.

If the Word of God referred to the factual claims within the Bible, then the true experts of the Word would be the academics who understand when these words were written, what the context was in which they were written, and what influences were at work in the composition. In addition to this, the legitimacy of the Word of God would always rest upon the answers one gave to questions such as when the earliest accounts of Jesus' life were written, whether or not they were recorded by eyewitnesses, whether there was a political agenda at work, whether the information in the text matches up with what we know about historical and geographical data, and so on.

What happens when the depth of the text is thought to be swallowed up in a rational approach like this is an externalization and objectification of faith. Here the words are analyzed, contextualized, and grasped by those who are not necessarily taken up by the depth of the event housed within them. Like someone who analyzes a parable without ever touching upon its transformative power, a purely academic understanding of the text, however brilliant, will always be a (mis)understanding. To believe that the words are the Word reduces the text to what can be named, described, and transcribed. To treat it in this way means that we approach the Word as a thing that stands before us to be examined, poked, prodded, and played with. The Word of God, in this reading, thus refers to something, some thing, some set of *things*.

The idea that faith involves engaging in an ongoing transformative dialogue instead of seeking some static, final understanding of God and the world can be seen to inform the Jewish anecdote that speaks about a young man who is seeking out an old and learned rabbi to be schooled in the wisdom of Hebraic logic. The story goes that after a prolonged search the young man finally finds a suitable rabbi and asks if the rabbi would be willing to tutor him. But upon seeing this youth the rabbi simply smiles and says, "You are too young and have too little life experience for the lessons that I have to teach. Come back to me in ten years."

But the young man is full of a confidence that borders on arrogance and so responds, "I may be young but I have already mastered Aristotelian logic and symbolic logic. Test me. Ask me any question you want and I will prove to you that I am ready."

The rabbi thinks for a few moments and then chooses a question: "Two men descend a chimney. When they get to the bottom, one man's face is covered in soot. Tell me, which one washes his face?"

In response the young man immediately says, "Why, that is easy. It would be the one with the soot on his face."

In response the rabbi turns to leave, saying, "Of course not. What are you thinking? It is the man without the soot who washes his face, for he sees his friend's complexion and thinks that he too must be dirty."

"Please don't send me away," replies the young man. "Test me again. Any question at all."

And so the rabbi thinks for a moment and then says, "OK, listen carefully this time. Two men descend a chimney. When they get to the bottom, one man's face is covered in soot. Tell me, which one washes his face?"

"Why, the man without the soot on his face," replies the young man.

Again the rabbi shakes his head, "You are not listening in the right way. It is obvious that it is the man with the soot on his face who washes. He sees the reaction of his friend upon reaching the ground, can taste the soot from his lips, and can feel it stinging his eyes. Now leave me in peace."

"Please," replies the young man, "test me one last time, as I think I have it now."

"One last time," replies the rabbi. "This time I want you to really listen. Two men descend a chimney. When they get to the bottom, one man's face is covered in soot. Tell me, which one washes his face?"

"The first answer I gave," shouts the young man, "but for different reasons."

"No, no, no," says the rabbi as he leaves. "They both wash their faces. How could someone descend a chimney and not think that their face would be covered in soot?"

Here we encounter the idea that before the young man could ever begin training in the deep wisdom of the tradition he must first learn how to give up the desire to reduce truth to some single, defined, unchanging, propositional system. He must learn to dialogue, to debate, to rethink, to critique.

Only then can he begin the journey toward a mode of religious understanding that goes deeper than epistemological insight (the realm of the scientific disciplines)—discovering a truth more profound than mere intellectual claims.

It is all too common for Christians to attempt to do justice to the scriptural narrative by listening to it, learning from it, and attempting to extract a way of viewing the world from it. But the narrative itself is asking us to approach it in a much more radical way. It is inviting us to wrestle with it, disagree with it, contend with it, and contest it—not as an end in itself, but as a means of approaching its life-transforming truth, a truth that dwells within and yet beyond the words.

And so, in our desire to remain absolutely, totally, and resolutely faithful to the Word of God, we come face to face with the idea that we must be prepared to wrestle with, question, and even betray the words. Only when we have broken with our initial naïveté and have embraced a passionate, critical engagement with the text can we ever hope to enter into that second naïveté and be embraced by the truth that is affirmed there.

PART 2

THE BEING OF GOD

FOUR

FOUR

The Name of God

In the previous section we explored how fidelity to the words of Scripture requires that we be prepared to constantly wrestle with and rethink them, for while they communicate indirectly about the divine Word, they do not render this Word present as an object for contemplation or analysis.

This relationship between the words and the Word could be compared to the relationship between the flesh of a person and that person's interior world. If we think that a person can be adequately understood as a purely biological system then we do an injustice to that person's subjectivity, while if we seek to move beyond the flesh of a person and engage in some "pure" relationship unsullied by their physical manifestation then we abuse and devalue that person's actual presence. The flesh is both our means of encountering the other and the barrier that prevents full exposure to the other's subjectivity. The exteriority of the other's flesh acts as a type of semi-permeable membrane that allows a type of partial access to the subjectivity of the other, exposing the other in an oblique and partial manner, as if through a glass darkly.

Truth as object

The elusive and foreign nature of this Word makes it difficult for us to let it speak its truth on its own terms. Part of the reason we find it so hard to let this Word reveal itself as it is rather than as we imagine it to be relates to the intellectual presuppositions that we have unwittingly inherited from our Western philosophical tradition, particularly in relation to our idea of truth. The idea of truth that we accept today is so ingrained in our psyche that it is hard to actually stand back and reflect upon other possible ways of thinking about the notion. However, the biblical text itself seems to be hinting at a different understanding of truth, one that questions the ubiquitous interpretation that we take for granted today. This idea of truth is so radical it places the entire philosophical roots of our society and the contemporary church into question.

At a very basic level, truth, as we commonly employ it, addresses anything that shows itself to us as an object for contemplation. Now, things show themselves to us in a variety of ways. For instance, a sunset is made present to us in a different way from that of a mathematical formula, while a mathematical formula appears to us in a different way from that of a historical event. In addition to this, some truths can be termed necessary because they cannot be otherwise (for example two plus two will always equal four) while others are called contingent, meaning that we can imagine a world where they would not be the case (for example, while people exist I can imagine an alternative universe in which they would not). All of these realms (historical, mental, necessary, and contingent) share something very important in common, namely that they each affirm a space within which objects appear (whether they be internal thoughts, historical events, contingent happenings, or necessary facts).

The idea that truth refers to the realm of appearance and contemplation means that truth is fundamentally connected to anything that can be distanced from us in some way. The idea of distance refers to the notion that truth implies the existence of a subject who is separate from the object (whether physical or mental) that the subject is contemplating.

We can see this idea of truth at work within the various academic disciplines. Within the university each area of academic study focuses its attention upon something that is taken to show itself in some manner: sociology studies society, history studies texts, psychology studies mental phenomena, biology studies organic systems, and so on.

Within the church as much as within the academy, we have been deeply influenced by the idea that for something to be true, it must show itself in the world, opening itself up to contemplation in some way. Truth, including religious truth, is thus related to the world of objects, to the world of facts. The result is a belief that we can distill the truth of faith into various sacraments, creeds, doctrines, historical interpretations, and even scientific theories, all of which are able to do justice to the claims of these ancient writings. The Word is taken to be some*thing* (the words of Scripture) that we can assess and interpret (stretching and distorting it until it becomes intelligible to us).

The net result is that we approach the Bible as something that can be analyzed and assessed, much as a sociologist contemplates society or a biologist reflects upon organic systems. It involves interpreting the meaning of, and then rationally assessing, such things as the possibility of miracles, the existence of Jesus, his death on a cross, his subsequent resurrection, and his ascension into heaven. In this way Christianity is judged to be true or false depending upon whether *our interpretation* of various biblical claims describes factual historical events.

The almost universal embrace of this approach concerning truth ensures that both those who embrace Christianity and those who do not universally assess it in terms of whether certain ideas concerning the world, God, and salvation are correct or incorrect, plausible or implausible, confirmed or placed into question by empirical data. The job of the Christian apologist is thus to show that religious claims can be accepted as possible, plausible, or even compelling.

There are numerous ways in which apologists for the faith will attempt to render their faith into an object that can be reflected upon and defended. This will generally involve a mix of basic philosophical reason, appeal to scriptural claims, and reference to personal religious experience. Each of these, while different, is combined in a potent mix that presents the truth of Christianity as something that can in some way be thought, touched, heard, or seen. Regardless of whether someone believes that the central claims of Christianity are true or false, likely or unlikely, what almost everyone seems to agree about is that the claims of Christianity are related to the realm of appearance (a realm in which we can distance ourselves from the issue in question and reflect upon it).

If the claims of Christianity are not open to being assessed in this way, the only alternative would seem to involve rejecting them as meaningless, a view that was developed by the philosophical tradition called Logical Positivism. This movement argued that if something is not able to be judged true or false, likely or unlikely, then we are rationally compelled to ignore it as irrelevant. For example, Logical Positivists would say that if someone claims that God exists but cannot be seen, heard, or experienced, then this is much like saying that pixies exist but cannot be seen, heard, or experienced, a statement that is not even worthy of being considered as true or false (for how would one go about proving or disproving it?). While Logical Positivism as a philosophical system was short-lived, its influence continues to be felt everywhere we turn. Indeed, its views on truth can be seen at work in the heart of much discussion concerning religion today. For instance, Richard Dawkins, Christopher Hitchens, and Daniel Dennett are all popular examples of thinkers who embrace a version of this common-sense realist outlook. It is precisely this approach to faith that postmodern religious thinkers question and critique as philosophically untenable, religiously problematic, and biblically unjustified.

The result of this view of truth is expressed in the never-ending repetition of discussions concerning whether or not there is evidence for thinking that God exists and that the claims concerning such things as the acts of Jesus are historical. Such a way of thinking about the truth of faith is so embedded in our religious thinking that the truth claims of Christianity are presented as offering us facts concerning the world (physics), humanity (anthropology), and God (metaphysics).

Lilith and the naming of God

This way of thinking about the truth of faith has a long history. For the remainder of this chapter we will show how this view has been expressed in different forms over time. A prime place to begin this exploration lies in the ancient Jewish legend, of unknown origin, that speaks of the first two human beings to ever grace the fertile grounds of Eden. While the Torah informs us that Adam and Eve were the first humans on the planet, this little-known apocryphal story, passed through countless generations via the cryptic and clandestine wisdom of a few rabbinical storytellers, offers an alternative reading.

According to archaic folklore, Eve was not the first woman to walk the earth but rather the second. It is said that the first woman, while never actually mentioned in the Torah, is hinted at within its pages via her ghostly, nuclear shadow.[35] It is said that we can perceive this shadow if we pay attention to a hairline fracture within the creation account,[36] occurring between the verses that tell us of the creation of male and female on the sixth day and those that inform us of the *subsequent* creation of Eve once Adam had named all the animals and become somewhat forlorn.[37] This fissure within the narrative proved fertile soil for the mythological imaginings of a few Midrash[38] storytellers who, perhaps inspired by the ghosts of their own lost loves and wrestling with the evil that lurked in the dark recesses of their own hearts, painted an extravagant picture around campfires of Adam's little-known companion, a companion who became his first, last, and most sacred of secrets: a woman so wild and wanton that God and Adam conspired together in a secret pact that ensured her name would never by uttered by them again.

This mysterious and independent woman went by the name of Lilith but has also been called the queen of demons, the sole seducer of YHWH, and the absolute sovereign of the *Sitra Ahra*.[39] Seldom is she spoken of and only rarely will anyone glimpse her name, for it is said that she has no dwelling place in the language and logic of mankind. She is described as too feral and independent a woman to be named and tamed by human discourse or dominated and domesticated through the domain of human reason, and so she dwells in the margins of our understanding, arising only as a sinister fairy tale, told in the dead of night, by Jewish parents who wish to frighten their wayward children. "Watch out," they whisper, "for if you are bad then Lilith will creep, sneak, and slither into your room to steal you away."

Around open fires late at night wise old rabbis would tell their listeners of an earth-shattering tragedy that befell the tranquil Garden of Eden. They would speak of how Adam had secretly feared Lilith, and of how his heart became a dwelling place for dark fantasies in which he would imagine ruling over her as a lord rather than dwelling with her as a lover. Eventually, so the story goes, he succumbed to this inner, festering darkness and late one evening demanded that Lilith lie beneath him during sexual intercourse. Disaster followed the verbalization of his desire, for Lilith resolutely refused, insisting that they were each formed from the dust of the earth and were therefore equal under the all-seeing gaze of God. The argument persisted and the relationship disintegrated. By trying to possess her he set in motion a series of disastrous events that would end with his losing her.

Shortly after this conflict Lilith hatched a plan that would enable her to escape the confines of Adam and Eden forever. Early one evening, as the sun was setting high in the sky, she found her creator walking alone in the gardens. Lilith carefully approached and instigated a conversation. After a little time had passed she leaned in close and whispered, "Please tell me your name, your secret name that remains hidden in the depths of your heart." God paused momentarily and then, in a moment of weakness, disclosed the name. Upon hearing it Lilith turned away and spoke it aloud. At that very instant she sprouted vast, mighty wings and flew high into the night sky, escaping the oppression of Adam's desire forever. According to some legends she returned, in an altogether different, more serpentine guise, to try and free Eve. And so, according to this little-known legend, it was not Eve who brought discord into the tranquil Garden of Eden but rather Adam.

Naming God

The key to understanding this haunting Jewish legend lies in the ancient belief that God possessed a secret name, a name that, if discovered, would enable the possessor to harness divine power. This name was not a mere word that pointed toward an object, as a signpost directs us toward a city, nor was it like the names that are given to us arbitrarily at birth, names that bring an individual to mind but that have no descriptive power. Rather it was a word that was believed to somehow place the very essence of God into human language.

This idea can still be perceived within the Kabbalistic tradition of Judaism in which we find reflections on the Monogrammata (the one-letter names of God), the Diagrammata (the two-letter names of God), the famous Tetragrammaton (the four-letter name of God), the Octagrammaton (an eight-letter name of God), and the Decagrammaton (a ten-letter name of God). In addition to this we find within the Kabbalistic tradition reflections on the twelve, fourteen, twenty-two, thirty-three, forty-two, and two hundred and sixteen-letter names of God; all of which pale into insignificance when compared to the massive three hundred and four thousand, eight hundred and five-letter name.[40]

The story of Ra and Isis

Such a mythology of the name is not restricted to the early Jewish mystical tradition but can be seen operating within a variety of cultures. An important example of this can be found in Egyptian mythology. One such myth revolves around the story of Isis and the Sun god, Ra. In ancient Egyptian thought, the creator ruled all deities and mortals in the guise of Ra. This god was known by many names, but none of these was his true name; his true name was concealed deep in his stomach to ensure that no sorcerer would ever discover it and wield it against him.

There was, however, one who dared to challenge the authority of Ra: his daughter Isis, who was described as more rebellious than a million men, more beautiful than a million gods and more to reckon with than a million spirits. Isis' husband, Osiris, was ruler over the Land of the Dead, but he longed to rule over the Earth. In order to help her husband, Isis set in motion a plan that would enable her to extract the name of Ra and thus gain the power required to overthrow him. Each day Ra would travel across his kingdom from the East to the West. Because Ra was old he would often stop during his travels in order to rest and drink some water. Isis noticed that Ra's hand would tremble as he drank, and that some of the water in his mouth would spill out. One day she collected some of the water that had spilled and mixed it with mud in order to create the form of a snake with a hood around its head like the crown of Ra. Then she placed this lifeless form strategically at a junction in the road where Ra passed on his daily travels. When Ra reached the junction he saw the snake and, intrigued by its hood, picked it up, saying, "cobra." Because Ra was such a powerful god he was able to bring things to life merely by speaking their names, so the snake began to wriggle around. Before he could set it down the snake bit him, causing a deep fever to descend. In response, Ra let out a piercing cry that rallied all the gods to his aid. The various deities were confused by what had happened but were powerless to help. Indeed, Ra was also powerless, because he had not created this creature but had merely given it life. The story goes that Isis then approached and promised that she could heal him if he were only to give her his secret name. Eventually, as the pain worsened, Ra reluctantly revealed his name. By possessing this name, Isis was then able to take her place among the most powerful of the Egyptian gods and goddesses.[41]

Moses and the burning bush: the scriptural naming of God

Moses, as one who had grown up in Egypt, would have been well-versed in this story and the idea of secret names, a fact that may well help us to understand the deeper meaning of his initial encounter with God in the arid wastelands of the Midian desert. We come across this encounter in the opening pages of Exodus, where we read that Moses is confronted by a divine call emanating from a burning bush. In response to hearing his name, Moses replies, "Here I am."[42]

In these words we witness the unconditional openness of Moses to the one who calls. After this response, Moses learns that the one who speaks is the God of Abraham, the God of Isaac, and the God of Jacob. He is then informed that he has been chosen to be the vessel through which the Abrahamic covenantal relationship will continue: he has been chosen to free the enslaved Israelites from Pharaoh's tyranny.

It is now, when faced with this monumental task, that Moses' initial, unconditional proclamation shows signs of wavering. Yet, judging that it would be neither prudent nor wise to question God directly, he summons up his strength and asks, "Who am *I*, that I should go to Pharaoh and bring the Israelites out of Egypt?"

Rather than focus upon Moses' ability to carry out the task, God responds with a promise: "I will be with you." Yet this is not enough for Moses. Still unconvinced about accepting this immense task and still skeptical that this promise of presence will be enough when faced with Pharaoh's formidable army, he attempts a different strategy: "Suppose I go to the Israelites and say to them, 'The God of your fathers has sent me to you,' and they ask me, 'What is his name?' *Then what shall I tell them?*"[43]

Here we can see that Moses is looking for more than some common name.[44] After all, he already knows whom it is that he is being addressed by. Instead, the writer is presenting us with someone who is seeking the secret, sacred name of God, a name that will wield unheard-of power, power that will be able to overthrow even the Pharaoh himself, power that will enable a stuttering old man to carry out the world-historical task that is being asked.

In response to this query concerning the Name, God replies with the enigmatic phrase *'ehyeh 'asher 'ehyeh*, a term that, since the Septuagint,[45] has generally been interpreted as a noun and translated into English as "I AM WHO I AM." Thus we read that God said to Moses, "I AM WHO I AM. This is what you are to say to the Israelites: 'I AM has sent me to you.'"[46]

The difference between this narrative and that dealing with Lilith is that Moses does not appear to be better off after hearing this phrase. He does not magically take on some divine power and wield it under the influence of his own will. So what can we make of this situation? One common reading is that the narrative is pointing out that the God of the Israelites cannot be controlled like the Egyptian deities. While Ra can be manipulated, the God of Abraham, Isaac, and Jacob is beyond such witchcraft. In this story God is presented as so unconcerned about giving out the name that we read this reply to Moses, ". . . say to the Israelites, 'I AM' has sent me to you," in effect saying, "Tell as many people as you want." The narrative is thus interpreted as representing the Israelites' God as infinitely greater than the gods and goddesses of Egypt precisely because the Israelites' God cannot be manipulated through sorcery and thus has no fear of disclosing the secret name. So in contrast to the mythology of Lilith and Ra we are confronted with a God who cannot be manipulated or tricked, a God whose power cannot be put into the hands of mere humans.

But while this story suggests that the divine name is not open to abuse by mortals, such a reading lends itself to the idea that the name may well offer us a way of gaining some understanding of God. The name may not bestow the possessor with magical power, but it may offer us some kind of descriptive insight.

The theological naming of God

This project of approaching God as an object that can be named gained credibility within the theological tradition of Western Christianity with Augustine who believed that the revelation of God as "I AM" told us something substantial about the one encountered in the life of faith. Greek philosophy had long been interested in the philosophical idea of "Being," the name given to the source of everything that is. Greek thought attempted to reflect upon this mysterious substance and say something substantive about it. For Augustine the God of the Hebrews was, in the proclamation of the "I AM," being revealed as the source that the Greeks had been reflecting upon all along. Here the phrase "I AM" was taken to suggest, not that God is a being like us, but that God could be described as the highest being, a being who is total, complete, and without need of explanation. In philosophical terms this phrase can be said to be a mythological way of describing God's existence as uncaused and necessary—ideas that have fueled various philosophers' and theologians' reflections on God ever since. Such reflections meant that God, as a being, could be rendered into something of thought. For when God is thought of as a being, albeit as the highest being, the great I AM, God is implicitly thought of as an object that may be contemplated.

During the high Middle Ages this idea was firmly established under the influence of the theologian Duns Scotus. Scotus lived and worked in the late thirteenth and early fourteenth centuries and is considered to be among the most influential thinkers of his era. He argued that God and humans share something very basic and important in common, namely the fact that both exist. However, while human beings only happen to exist, God exists by necessity. This simply means that while we could easily never have been born, God has to exist and could never not exist.

Not only is our existence contingent (we just happen to exist) but so are the various ways in which we exist. For example, certain facts such as one's height, hair color, and weight could conceivably have been different. What we are comes into existence, changes over time, and goes out of existence. For Scotus, however, God must be thought of as necessary and unchanging. Yet despite the differences between people and the divine, Scotus argued that both God and humanity have "being" in common, a fact that ensures that there is a similarity between ourselves and God that allows us to speak meaningfully about God. While it was not believed that this naming can magically give us access to the power of God, such thinking claimed to give us an insight into the essence of God.

Such an approach affirmed a direct correlation between our understanding of God and God's essence. Instead of thinking about our understanding of God as a poetic utterance arising from an encounter with God it was thought that our understanding of God directly matched up with the very nature of God. While the former approach argues that our understanding is an acknowledged misunderstanding that arises in the aftermath of God, the later approach argues that these words can render God rationally manifest.

God as greatest conceivable being:
the philosophical naming of God

Having mentioned some examples of naming God in apocryphal legend, Scripture, and theology, I wish to conclude this chapter by showing how the naming of God was solidly inscribed into the very fabric of modern thinking through the philosophical work of one of the most influential thinkers of the Enlightenment, the philosopher René Descartes. Frustrated by many of the never-ending philosophical and theological discussions that he had grown up with, Descartes famously sought a new foundation upon which to base philosophical thought, one that was simple, clear, and indubitable.

In order to do this he set about doubting everything that it was possible to doubt with the hope of finding an idea so certain, so absolute, that it would provide a foundation for the development of a philosophy that could withstand the most ferocious attacks of skepticism. As such, he sought one fixed and immovable point from which to build a solid philosophical fortress, an "Archimedean point" so clear and distinct that it could not, in any way, be doubted. In order to find this starting point he embraced the most all-encompassing skepticism. Yet, far from sinking into this murky world where nothing is known, Descartes found that he could only slide so far, discovering what he believed to be one thing that could not be swallowed up by the seemingly all-consuming sludge of skepticism, one fact that could provide a sure footing on which humans could found their knowledge.

He found that while it was possible to doubt his perception of the external world, the existence of other minds, and even our most basic ideas about the world (for he postulated that there may be an all-powerful demon who ensures that all our most basic beliefs are always misdirected) there was one thing that was utterly impossible for him to doubt, namely the fact that he was thinking. For when he tried to doubt that he was thinking, he found that he was thinking about doubt. To think that he was not thinking was simply to think about not thinking. Thus he could not think that he was not thinking without, well, thinking. As such he declared that it was impossible for him to doubt that he was thinking, and that such thinking proved beyond all doubt that he must exist. Hence he came up with his "principle of principles," the point from which he believed that he could finally formulate a method that would be able to separate the wheat of truth from the chaff of falsehood, the "Archimedean point" that would enable him to lift the world out of the darkness of ignorance and into the light of reason—*Cogito, ergo sum* (I think, therefore I am).

Remaining in the guise of a skeptic, Descartes continued to doubt everything else (the existence of the world, other minds, God, etc.), but he could not doubt that he thought and thus he could not doubt that he existed. He argued that even if an all-powerful demon does indeed rule the universe, ensuring that we are deceived in all things at all times, this demon is unable to deceive us about the reality of our own existence, at least if we follow Descartes' method. For instance, we could all theoretically inhabit a universe like that envisaged by the Wachowski brothers in the film *The Matrix*. However, no matter how hard they tried, the machines that had constructed this artificial world would never be able to deceive us about the reality of our own existence. No matter what artificial construct they created, the fact of our existence would remain as the one indubitable fact where the wool could never be pulled over our eyes.

On the basis of this foundation Descartes went on to argue that we could prove the existence of God.[47] Unlike other arguments that attempted to prove God, arguments that relied upon physical reality (such as the existence and nature of the world), Descartes claimed that the mind alone was sufficient. In order to demonstrate this he began by pointing out the fact that, as thinking beings, we are confronted by a whole menagerie of thoughts. He pointed out that although these thoughts may not relate to anything that exists in the real world (i.e., the thoughts we have may have no connection with what, if anything, lies beyond our mind), their existence, as thoughts, cannot be denied. In other words, while I can legitimately doubt that other people actually exist I cannot doubt that I have thoughts of other people existing.

He then went on to note that we have thoughts concerning a variety of inanimate objects, animals, and even supernatural beings. All of these could conceivably have been dreamed up by the mind itself. Yet, in addition to these ideas he argued that we also have an implicit idea of God.[48] When we think of God, Descartes pointed out, we think of an "infinite, independent, supremely intelligent, supremely powerful [being], and the creator of myself and anything else that may exist."[49] Descartes went on to argue that this idea could not possibly have been dreamed up by our own mind because something cannot create that which is beyond its ability to create.

He argued that the thought of God (as infinite and unlimited) is so fundamentally different and superior to our understanding of ourselves (as finite and limited) that it stands utterly beyond the ability of the mind to create: just as a cat could not think up the theory of general relativity, so a human mind could not think up the nature of God.[50]

At this point Descartes asked where the idea of God could possibly have originated from, for while it is possible for finite beings to conceive of finite things, it would, he argued, be utterly impossible for us to possess a clear and distinct idea of some infinite substance without its having been originally produced by a source capable of implanting such a notion. To answer his own question, Descartes pointed out that, in the same way that a finite mind could only create finite thoughts, only an infinite mind could conceive of the infinite. Hence the only possible source for such a thought is indicated by the idea itself: *the idea of an infinite, independent, supremely intelligent, and supremely powerful being must have been produced by something that is itself infinite, independent, supremely intelligent, and supremely powerful.* Hence he concluded that God must necessarily exist, for only God could have implanted that idea in our minds. In short, the argument can be broken down in the following manner:

1. A finite mind can only form finite ideas.
2. We possess an idea of God as infinite.
3. This idea must therefore have been put there by something other than ourselves.
4. Whatever placed the idea of God into our minds must be capable of forming the idea itself.
5. Only an infinite being could form this infinite thought.
6. This infinite being is what we call God.
7. Therefore God must exist.

The point of describing Descartes' thought here is simply to draw out how his argument rested on the assumption that we have an innate idea of God. His conclusion was that any reasonable individual will be able to gain insight into the nature of God simply by reflecting upon an image that is already implanted in that individual's mind.

The contemporary church

This outline of examples derived from mythology, Scripture, theology, and philosophy is designed to show that there has been a long and varied tradition that has been interested in articulating the name of God, of speaking about God as a being like other beings, albeit the greatest being. When this idea is imported into Christianity the assumption is then made that God's existence and nature are offered to the mind via revelation.[51] In this way the Bible is approached as a type of divine textbook that provides us with information concerning God. Such thinking continues today in churches that assert that we can know God and the mind of God to some degree so long as we follow the correct, spirit-inspired interpretation of Scripture. Even though the believer will point out that we see through a glass darkly, it will be claimed that we can say something substantive about the source of our faith via the presence of creation, Scripture, and religious experience. Indeed, it is claimed that if we were not held back by our own intellectual limits and sin then the source of faith would become even more visible to us, for it is our own limits that hold us back from grasping God rather than something fundamental about the nature of God.

Such a view holds forth the idea that while there is a concealed side of God that lies beyond our understanding, there is also a manifest side, and our knowledge of the latter is to be deepened, protected, and promoted. Knowingly betraying our knowledge of God (the revealed side) would amount to a willful turning from the life of faith. However, as we will explore shortly, instead of thinking about there being a cut between the revealed and the concealed side of God, the Incarnation teaches us that there is a much more radical cut at work in Christianity, namely a cut that slices right through the revealed side of God. This cut of radical unknowing ensures that even what is revealed remains concealed. It ensures that the opening of God into the world remains an ineffable mystery in its very occurrence.

FIVE

Eclipsing God

God's name as a noun

In the story of Lilith we are not privy to what God whispers as God and Lilith rest together in the cool of the garden. The secret name may well have been revealed to Lilith, but it was not revealed to us. However, as we move far beyond that secluded garden nestled near the waters of the Euphrates and turn toward the Midian desert thousands of years later, we encounter a rather different scenario. It would seem that enough time has passed for God to have forgotten what had transpired in Eden all those years before. Here, when Moses asks for the name, God answers yet again, but this time the name is recorded for all to see. Here is no secret whisper between intimate friends; instead, God proclaims the name and even tells Moses to go and share it with the Israelites.

As we have already witnessed, a popular reading of this episode points to the idea that, although this name tells us something about God, it cannot be misused by sorcerers and spell casters. What we can get from this name is an insight into the nature of God, namely, that God exists necessarily, absolutely, and without limit. By saying that God exists in this way, one is saying that the word *God* and the idea of existence are intertwined in much the same way that the word "triangle" and the idea of a three-sided shape are. In the same way that the statement "a triangle has three sides" is necessarily true, so too is the statement "God exists": this idea has had philosophers debating for millennia.[52]

In this reading the ideas of existence, manifestation, and reflection are all intertwined: God exists, God has manifested this existence to us, and so we can mediate upon it. This way of thinking about the source of faith is so embedded in our thinking that it often seems impossible for us to consider the possibility that the source and truth of faith is something other than an object of contemplation. It seems ridiculous for us to even postulate the possibility of this source's being made manifest as existing beyond the categories of something and nothing, of this source's manifesting itself as *some(no)thing*.

The mythology of Lilith in the garden of Eden, the scriptural description of Moses by the burning bush, the theological work of Duns Scotus, and the philosophical method of Descartes each manifest different ways in which God is viewed as an object of contemplation. Each seeks to ground faith in naming.

This desire has so infested Christian thought today that the truth of Christianity is viewed as connected to a series of objective facts about this source, facts that can be reflected upon, defended, and attacked. We can see this clearly when we consider how creationists understand the truth of faith. It is popular within the scientific community to contrast the theory of evolution with the creationist's interpretation of Genesis as a six-day (or six-epoch) act of creation, pointing out that the former is properly scientific while the latter is not. However, this approach misses the profound similarities that actually exist between the creationist and evolutionary accounts of the world. In response to the claim that they are not scientific, creationists are quick to point out that they actually affirm the same scientific worldview as those who affirm evolution, a claim backed up by the fact that some of their institutions spend vast sums of money in an attempt to defend their faith in the same way that one would defend a certain view on the structure of atoms in physics or a cellular structure in microbiology.

At a very basic level the creationist judges the truth of faith as a factual claim that can be externalized from the one considering it, objectified, and dispassionately reflected upon. For the creationist the truth affirmed by Christianity can then, in principle, be proven via the same empirical processes as those embraced in classical scientific theory, because it is fundamentally of the same substance as the objects studied in science. Of course, the creationist can be seen to engage in bad science, and this is no doubt what evolutionary biologists are reacting against. My point here, however, is not related to the debate itself but rather to how the creationist's approach to religious truth presupposes that the truth of faith is on the same level as scientific statements. In philosophical terms one would say that the creationist is claiming the same ontological status for both the claims of science and the claims of faith.

Beliefs such as a six-day creation, a fruit tree with the power to bestow knowledge of good and evil, a snake with the ability to talk, and Jesus ascending into heaven are all taken to be descriptions of historical facts that exist on the same mundane natural level as a phenomenon such as snow falling on a winter's evening. These events can then, in principle, be assessed on purely scientific grounds. For example, if a video camera existed at the beginning of the world, we could have recorded the snake chatting with Eve, or later, we could have captured an image of Jesus rising off the ground and leaving the atmosphere.

In the next chapter we will be asking if there is a way of thinking otherwise about the truth affirmed by Christianity, a way that is more appropriate to the life of faith and radical kernel of the Christian message. However, before doing so we need to address why such an alternative is needed. We must ask what is so wrong about thinking about the source of our faith as an object and of approaching religious truth as that which speaks directly about this source. Why is it problematic to approach revelation as offering us factual information concerning the world, humanity, and God? What are the consequences of approaching the truth affirmed by Christianity as an object open to rational reflection?

Creation of distance between believer and the source of the believer's faith

One of the results of thinking about the truth affirmed by Christianity as comprised of facts that can be externalized and reflected upon (i.e., as made up of substantive claims concerning God, the world, the ministry and person of Christ, and the status of the Bible) is that it introduces a distance between a person and that person's faith. The very idea of being able to reflect upon the truth of faith involves the need to create a critical distance between the thinker and what the thinker is thinking about. In this way a distinction is set up between the subject (the one who thinks) and the object (that which is being thought). This allows us to approach the truth of faith with a level of personal detachment and objectivity.

Yet, such an approach seems foreign to the unconditional commitment that is demanded of authentic believers, a commitment described by the apostle Paul as one that involves becoming a living sacrifice.[53] Distancing oneself from one's faith asks that believers engage with the deepest, most intimate, most personal, and most pressing issue in their lives in the guise of a detached, disinterested observer. Yet, approaching the truth affirmed by Christianity as some abstract, objective assertion to be tested, simply demonstrates that the questioner is approaching this query as a problem to be pondered, dissected, and solved, rather than a mystery to inhabit and be transformed by.

While approaching things in the world as objects to study and understand is vital for the development of technology, our faith cannot be treated as a detached object without fundamentally misunderstanding the nature of faith itself. The life of faith cannot be treated in the way we approach objects such as computers (which become more understandable the more we dissect and explore them). Persons of faith are not ones who act like rational detached individuals who are coldly assessing the evidence of their faith in the same way that a mathematician considers a formula. Believers are, as we shall explore in the next chapter, implicated in their faith, immersed in it, overwhelmed by it. This does not mean that they cannot think critically and rationally about their faith, but rather that the language of so much traditional theology and philosophy is the wrong language to use.

The truth of faith is handed over to the academic

Once the truth affirmed by Christianity is approached as an object to contemplate, it is treated as something that can be tested in the same way as any other propositional claim. This effectively gives the truth affirmed by Christianity over to the academic who has the space, time, and skills to contemplate these claims in depth. Philosophers can ask whether these claims are logically sound, historians can ponder the likelihood of certain scriptural claims, sociologists can ask whether Christian truth claims play a functional role in society, psychologists can explore whether these truth claims are only wish fulfillments, and theologians can contemplate the relationship of these truths to Christian doctrines and creeds.

In this way Christianity is given over to the scholar who sits at her desk, surrounded on all sides by an endless sea of ink, adding her own tiny drops so as to justify her living. The truth of Christianity is thus given over to those who can dissect it, study it, and reflect upon it.

The introduction of doubt as a corrosive enemy

When the truth affirmed by Christianity is thought of as constituting a series of factual claims open to being assessed by intellectual experts, Christianity opens itself up to a corrosive form of doubt that threatens to destroy it. Later I shall be exploring the deep importance of doubt in the life of faith. However, this importance can only be understood if we think of the truth affirmed by Christianity in a way that is freed from the realm of objectivity.

As soon as Christianity is thought of as something that makes claims to a set of facts that exist in the world, then it becomes subject to a whole range of critiques. This does not in any way imply that we must reject specific claims in the Bible, any more than it implies that we must embrace them; this is another question entirely, one that can be approached in relation to the best evidence that we have. It merely points out that if we take such claims as the "truth" of faith then we predicate that truth upon claims that will always be open to question. Of course within the Bible there are various claims to historical events; the point is that these claims, like all claims, are open to question, and so, if the truth of faith rests upon them, then it is also open to question.

Thus the truth affirmed by Christianity ends up being treated like any other set of factual claims, claims that are provisional and open to being proven wrong. Even if one believes that the various claims within the Bible are wholly accurate, it is always possible that a new discovery in archaeology, history, or biblical scholarship will overturn the current body of evidence. Apologetics, in its attempt to defend the factual claims of the Bible through the use of reason, thus implicitly affirms the very philosophical outlook that undermines its own project, placing the truth of Christianity in the realm of rational reflection and thus into the realm of reasonable doubt and provisionality.

This has the effect of placing the Christian idea of truth upon a very tentative and fragile foundation, one that could not possibly justify an individual's unconditional commitment—one that would not be able to embrace Jesus' statement that one ought to lay one's life down for one's faith. Such an approach to the truth affirmed by Christianity would effectively mean that the believer would have to bow down before the academic researchers who are able to discuss which biblical texts are authentic, when they where written, by whom, and for what purpose. The believer would need to study all the available evidence and ascertain facts such as whether or not the Gospels record the writings of people who were eyewitnesses to the events they mention, and if not, whether they knew the eyewitnesses.

To be a believer would thus require some hefty subscriptions to the latest academic journals in order to see if the truth claims of Christianity could still be regarded as plausible, or even possible. Philosophy journals would become a stable diet for the preacher who would, in fear and trembling, be working out whether belief in Christianity is still rational. Journals dealing with biblical scholarship would become the norm in home groups, and psychological journals would need to be read as an integral part of our devotional meditations (helping us to work out whether our religious experience was likely to have descended from heaven or whether it really welled up from the depths of our unconscious).

Divorce of knowledge from practice

In addition to these problems, such an approach creates a wedge between possessing "truth" and engaging in a life of devotion and service. Here, knowledge of God becomes something akin to the type of information a physicist would have concerning the nature of black holes. This type of knowledge does not require, evoke, or demand any moral practice. It does not matter that a particular physicist has had an affair or embezzled money, for regardless of the physicist's moral failures, the scientific knowledge the physicist possesses will be just as legitimate as if the physicist were a saint. In short, the truth at work in one's discipline has no direct relation to one's mode of existence. Yet this is foreign to the type of truth explored within the Judeo-Christian narrative, a truth that is profoundly related to the way that one operates in the world. For instance, what are we to make of the claim that those who love know God, while those who do not love do not know God?[54]

With the idea that the truth affirmed by Christianity can be grasped in a way that has no necessary relationship to one's engagement with the world, it becomes possible to have some kind of knowledge of God that is separated from the life of faith, that is, a life taken up in the liberating, revolutionary ministry exemplified in the way of Christ. The knowledge of religious truth can thus be gained and maintained outside of a transfigured life.

Religion as well-being

Following on from this, when the truth of faith is reduced to the idea of a theoretical system divorced from one's practice, then faith becomes associated with an affirmation of certain beliefs that seem to do little more than offer the believer a matrix of meaning with which to understand life. This effectively reduces Christianity to a set of claims concerning ideas such as the world's being created for a purpose, God's loving us, and the existence of heaven. The problem arises not when one accepts these beliefs but rather when one thinks that they are what constitutes the truth of faith.

Embracing certain beliefs as the truth of faith ensures that the meaning and purpose offered by Christianity becomes directly associated with claims concerning such things as the afterlife rather than a radical transformation that alters one's mode of being in the world. The argument is often made that Christianity provides meaning because it offers the idea of God as love and provides the vision of an eternal life. Yet, if this is the meaning that Christianity offers, then it is far from unproblematic. For instance, there is an ancient view that places this idea into question by arguing that the belief in the existence of a god who bestows eternal life would be the very thing that would drain life of all meaning. This idea is expressed in Wolfgang Petersen's *Troy* in which Achilles (Brad Pitt) says to Briseis (Rose Byrne), a temple acolyte of Apollo,

> I'll tell you a secret, something they didn't teach you in your temple. The gods envy us. They envy us because we're mortal, because every moment might be our last. Everything is more beautiful for the doomed.[55]

The point of this argument was to show that one cannot really experience some of the greatest human emotions if we are certain that everything will work out well in the end. For instance, how can we experience true heroism if there is nothing to lose? It was for this reason that the ancient Greeks valued the ability to embrace life in all its fragility. They did not view this as an impediment to life but as the prerequisite to really experiencing and enjoying it. Thus, in response to those who would say that life is truly meaningful only if we are sure that God exists, one could respond by saying that in actual fact our lives have meaning only if God does not exist.

It was Nietzsche who most passionately and insightfully attacked a Christianity that founded its notion of truth on the absolute affirmation of an eternal, static, changeless heavenly realm. Indeed, Nietzsche felt that it was such an affirmation of world without end that was nothing less than a form of nihilism, for the belief in eternal life robbed this life of its fragile, fleeting beauty.

My point here is not to argue for or against the existence of a heavenly eternity, but rather to help draw us away from the idea that such a belief relates to what Christianity offers as its transformative truth. Indeed, if one does believe in a literal heaven, it may even be important to suspend this belief in order to approach the truly good news of Christianity. For the original disciples the introduction of an afterlife arose only after they had already given up everything and followed Jesus—in short, after the good news had already been received.

By confusing such beliefs with the truth of faith we can begin to hold them in such an absolute and unreasonable way that they effectively become crutches that stop us from facing up to the uncertainties of existence. Uncertainties, doubts, and suffering are part of life, and thus they are part of faith (which is not an escape from life but a means of entering more fully into it). The truth of faith does not protect us from the unknowing and suffering of mere mortals; rather, it provides a means of living with the unknowing and suffering. This reality is testified to throughout the Bible and is particularly evident in the book of Psalms.

Within Christianity such doubts as we see expressed in the Psalms can be called experiences of Black Saturday, a name that is given to the day that is nestled between Good Friday and Easter Sunday, a day that symbolizes a radical uncertainty and unknowing: Where is Christ? Is he dead? Is death victorious? There is a sense in which we all dwell in the space of Black Saturday, that place of uncertainty, not a place between crucifixion and resurrection in which we wonder if Christ will return and death will be defeated, but in a place after the Resurrection in which we wonder if Christ did return and if death was defeated. Let us be courageous enough to face up to this reality, not only for its own sake but also so that we can begin to approach what the good news of Christianity really is.

The death of God

So far we have pointed out that if the truth that emanates from the Judeo-Christian tradition is the same as the idea of truth that we employ today, then it is a truth that (1) creates a distance between believers and what they believe, (2) is able to be truly judged only by the academic, (3) is one that is constantly under threat by doubt, (4) is only contingently related to a transformed life, and (5) can function purely as an ideological crutch that shields us from embracing life.

It was precisely this idea that Nietzsche attacked when he declared that God was dead in a famous philosophical parable written at the close of the nineteenth century. There are few philosophical phrases as well known or as misunderstood as this one. A brief survey of twentieth-century thought shows that it helped to inspire a wide diversity of philosophical movements. The parable itself reads as follows:

Haven't you heard of that madman who in the bright
morning lit a lantern and ran around the marketplace
crying incessantly, "I'm looking for God! I'm looking
for God!" Since many of those who did not believe in
God were standing around together just then, he caused
great laughter. Has he been lost then? asked one. Did he
lose his way like a child? asked another. Or is he hiding?
Is he afraid of us? Has he gone to sea? Emigrated?—
Thus they shouted and laughed, one interrupting the
other. The madman jumped into their midst and pierced
them with his eyes. "Where is God?" he cried; "I'll tell
you! *We have killed him*—you and I! We are all his
murderers. But how did we do this? How were we able
to drink up the sea? Who gave us the sponge to wipe
away the entire horizon? What were we doing when we
unchained this earth from its sun? Where is it moving
to now? Where are we moving to? Away from all suns?
Are we not straying as through an infinite nothing? Isn't
empty space breathing at us?"[56]

For Nietzsche the idea of God had become inextricably
linked with claims to do with the idea that there is an overall
meaning and purpose in the universe, that is, with factual
claims. Indeed, he judged this approach to be so embedded
in the culture of his time that anyone who believed that
the world had some overarching meaning accessible to the
human mind was actually affirming this God even if they
denied it (a claim that many religious apologists make today,
although for opposite reasons). For Nietzsche, this approach

was an expression of Descartes' philosophical God, and it reigned supreme both in the church and in the academy.

This helps to explain why the people who the madman is speaking to in the parable are actually described as not believing in God. For while they had given up on church, prayer, and even the word "God," they implicitly affirmed and were comforted by the idea of overall cosmic meaning. For Nietzsche God was dead, not because some entity "out there" had ceased to exist, but rather because the idea of God had become synonymous with Descartes' God, and Descartes' God had no positive transformative power. In other words, for Nietzsche God is nothing more than an idea that comforts the individual with the belief that the world has some overall meaning. God was directly affirmed by the believer and indirectly evoked by the so-called enlightened scientists of his day, but this belief had no real effect upon either of them. Such an intellectual belief did not evoke a radically transformed life of loving enemies, giving away worldly goods, and standing up against injustice. Belief in God was now just a type of crutch, an ideological system divorced from life. For Nietzsche God had gradually become nothing more than a guarantee of meaning, and this meaning seemed to serve no other purpose than the rather selfish one of making us feel secure in the universe.

If the traditional religious philosophers asked that we remain faithful to our objective understanding of God, Nietzsche asked that we betray such understandings because they offer us nothing but an ideological drug that enables us to live without embracing existence. Hence, Nietzsche equated drugs and religion, for both provide ways for the individual to avoid facing up to life in all its beauty and horror.

Nietzsche looked to a time when people would be able to live without such ideological crutches—a time when they could embrace life without this Cartesian God. This would not, however, signal the reign of some kind of traditional atheism, for if God had become synonymous with the affirmation of ultimate meaning, then Nietzsche was saying that the atheism of his day was still too interested in playing the same game, affirming a meaningful universe without God. Atheism had to embrace its own message and overcome itself, recognizing that there was no privileged position to judge what the world was all about either scientifically or religiously. Nietzsche was thus attempting to show how Cartesian theology lay deeply embedded within the thinking of modern Western philosophers and scientists, even though they often claimed to have nothing to do with theology. The time that he looked toward was one when people would simply accept the world as it is and create meaning from the raw materials of our everyday activities.

This was not an argument that God as a being did not exist any more than it was an argument for the existence of God. It was an argument that claimed that the question of God's existence was redundant. Until this time philosophers had often taken the question of whether the world was meaningful to be of fundamental importance. The thinking person was one who seriously asked the question *why*. However, Nietzsche responded, not by attempting to answer the question, but rather by undermining it entirely. In response to the question "Why?" he replied, "Why ask why?"

Toward a religionless Christianity

The problem that Nietzsche was pointing out was that once the truths of a religion such as Christianity are viewed as referring to certain facts, then what becomes important in faith is the embrace of certain beliefs that have no necessary connection with a passionate, moral life. This was something that Dietrich Bonhoeffer deeply understood and that caused him to write, near the end of his life, about the possibility of a religionless Christianity, a Christianity that rejects a faith that speaks only to those who cannot embrace existence without some kind of religious ideology. Bonhoeffer returned to the Scriptures in order to uncover a Christianity that is able to speak to the wide-eyed, intelligent adult in us, or indeed to rediscover a Christianity that can actually help to bring us into adulthood, rather than keeping us as infants.

In reading Nietzsche he too became concerned that Christianity had become an anemic ideological expression that not only appealed to the infant within humanity but that fundamentally stood in the way of our becoming strong, intelligent, and courageous human beings who reflect our dignity as being formed in the image of God. He wondered how to express the relevance of God (the God of faith) to those who do not feel the need for God (the Cartesian God that provides a matrix of meaning), while encouraging those who embrace such ideological religion to grow beyond it—helping those who have forsaken God (the Cartesian God) to find God (the God of faith) and those who have found God to forsake God.

By exploring these issues he was responding to the idea that Christianity for a long time has been aimed at responding to a need in people (such as the feeling of guilt). As such it has been expressed as good news that can only be heard once a person has been brought low by the bad news. This self-centered approach to the faith that he rejected is caricatured in an anecdote that speaks of two friends walking past a church that has a large sign that reads, "Become a Christian and receive $100." Upon seeing the strange advertisement one of the friends dares the other to go inside and get the money. The friend agrees and enters the building. After about half an hour he comes back out. "Well," says his friend, "did you get the cash?" In response the man looks down at his friend, shakes his head in disapproval, and replies, "Is money the only thing you non-Christians ever think about?"

How many of us have treated the gospel as an object that can answer a deep-seated need (for acceptance, happiness, companionship, a clear conscience), and in so doing have approached Christianity in self-interested weakness, hoping that it will be the pill that will cure us, the liquid solution that will provide the ultimate solution. Bonhoeffer wondered whether it is possible to embrace God out of love and lightness of heart, out of a seduction that is caught up in the call of God rather than the need of God.

This idea is analogous to someone who feels perfectly happy without a partner, content in his or her life and work, but who eventually comes across someone with whom they fall in love. Here the individual does not enter into the relationship out of need but out of love, and in the midst of it is able to claim, "I never needed you until now." It is in the presence of the other (not in the other's absence) that a need is formed. In the other, the need is born rather than abolished. Here we discover that the need that is born in love and faith is a retroactive need that comes after the encounter. Instead of the bad news coming before the good news it comes after it.

So the question that faces us now concerns what the truth affirmed by Christianity looks like if it is not bound up in an allegiance to some ideological system, when it is no longer reduced to a worldview that merely offers us a set of propositional statements.

SIX

Beyond God

Asking the wrong question

There is an old anecdote that speaks of a couple planning to decorate their living room with attractive but expensive wallpaper. It so happens that one of their friends had recently decorated one of their rooms with a similar material, a room that was of similar size to their own. So the couple decided to visit her house and ask how many rolls she had purchased. The woman replied that she had bought eight rolls of wallpaper. Satisfied with this answer, the couple purchased eight rolls themselves. However, by the time they were halfway through the fourth roll they had completed the room. Annoyed at the wasted money, they complained to their friend, saying, "We bought eight rolls of paper as you said, but we only needed four." "I know exactly how you feel," said their friend. "I had the same problem."

The moral of this story is that one should ask the right question in order to get the right answer. Instead of finding out how many rolls of wallpaper their friend bought, they should have asked how many rolls of wallpaper she used.

Today it would seem that, when it comes to the popular debates concerning Christianity, the wrong question is being asked. On one side of this debate we have individuals such as Richard Dawkins, Daniel Dennett, and Sam Harris arguing that the truth claims of Christianity are not valid, while on the other side there is an army of religious apologists publishing books in an attempt to prove them wrong. The debate itself has many interesting facets. However, the most fascinating aspect of this debate, as we have seen from the previous chapter, concerns the fact that, at a very basic level, both sides implicitly affirm the idea that the truth claims of Christianity take the form of assertions about reality that can reflected upon, considered, and judged according to reason and empirical research. It is assumed by both sides that the truth claims of Christianity involve assertions concerning such things as the accuracy of the Bible, whether a man named Jesus lived, whether or not the accounts of his life and works are accurate, whether miracles are possible, and whether religious experience points toward the existence of a concrete reality beyond the physical world. While the disagreements among the various protagonists of this debate can often be fierce, there is then a profound agreement among those involved. For on each side Christianity is to be judged via the idea of truth we described in the last chapter.

However, instead of asking the question concerning whether or not Christianity is true, it should be becoming clear that we must first ask a more basic and fundamental one, namely, "What is it that Christianity claims when it claims to be true?" If we do not ask this question, then we will end up naïvely assuming that the common understanding of truth upon which this debate is premised is the standard that ought to be used in order to judge the truth of the Judeo-Christian tradition.

Pascal and the critique of Descartes' God

In order to approach this question let us look at how we ought to consider the source of faith, namely that which we call God. In chapter four we explored how Descartes was one of the clearest philosophical examples of a thinker who believed that we could name God. Yet there where times when Descartes himself wondered whether this was really the case. For instance, at one point he wrote, "The idea of the infinite, if it is to be a true idea, cannot be grasped at all, since the impossibility of being grasped is contained in the formal definition of the infinite."[57] In other words, Descartes was openly wondering whether his definition of God was in fact a definition at all or, in actual fact, a way of saying that God cannot be defined. Here he was wondering whether his claim that *God is infinite* (a claim about God's nature and essence) actually leads to the conclusion that *God is incomprehensible* (a claim about what we can actually know about God). Indeed this is one of the recurring critiques of his *Meditations*. For instance, Thomas Hobbes noted that,

God is conceived as *infinite*; that is, I cannot conceive or imagine limits to him, or uttermost parts beyond which I can image none further; but from this it follows that the term *infinite* gives rise to an idea not of God's infinity but of my own bounds and limits . . . to say God is *infinite* is just to say that he belongs to the class of things whose bounds are not conceivable. This rules out any idea of God; what sort of idea can be without origin and without bounds?[58]

Thus, for Hobbes, Descartes' definition of God as an "infinite, independent, supremely intelligent, supremely powerful [being] and the creator of myself and anything else that may exist," actually turned out to be a way of claiming that God was beyond definition. In short, the idea that God is infinite was, for Hobbes, a way of saying that God is beyond any ideas we can come up with: to say that God is infinite is to say that God is not finite and thus to make a merely negative claim. To make this claim is thus to really say nothing concrete at all about God but rather to offer up a veiled means of commenting upon the finitude of the one who speaks—it is a description of our own limits. It was left to a religious contemporary of Descartes to really drive this point home. The great mathematician and religious thinker Blaise Pascal possessed a keen insight into the limited nature of our rational systems and the idolatrous nature of extrapolating upon the existence and essence of God from our finite and fragile location. For instance, in his reflections upon the "disproportion in man" Pascal reflected upon our position in the universe by commenting on how a serious reflection upon the glory of the heavens will lead us to understand that "the earth is a mere speck compared to the vast orbit descended by [the sun]" and that "this vast orbit itself [is] no more than the tiniest point compared to that described by the stars revolving in the firmament."[59] Pascal argued that the imagination would first "grow weary of conceiving things before nature tires of producing them."[60]

In addition to this he wrote that each minute atom in the universe itself contains an infinity beyond measure, inviting us to imagine a "new abyss" that exists in the atom whereby "an infinity of universes, each with its firmament, its planets, its earth, in the same proportions as in the visible world, and on that earth animals, and finally mites, in which he will find again the same results as in the first."[61] Through such reflections he drew out the extent to which we stand as a giant over one infinite expanse, while being dwarfed in relation to another. In relation to the universe he argued that we are a "nothing, a middle point between all and nothing, infinitely remote from an understanding of the extremes"; thus "the end of things" lies in "impenetrable secrecy."[62] In this way he argued that it is quite beyond our faculties to possess an adequate notion of nature, let alone its source.

By drawing out our finite limitations Pascal undermined Descartes' attempt at gaining a tiny platform of absolute knowledge (the existence of the thinker) in order to expose the infinitely large (God), pointing out that both the minute and the massive stretch into ineffable darkness before us. In contradistinction to Descartes, he argued that humanity exists at sea level, held between the heavenly realm of "certain knowledge" and eerie depths of "absolute ignorance."[63]

Yet none of these ideas led Pascal away from faith or from God, they simply helped him expose what was problematic about the approach of those around him and enabled him to approach God as a truth that is revealed to us outside the confines of knowledge.

Reception without conception

In order to approach this idea of truth beyond knowledge, let us return to Moses in the Midian desert. We have already noted that one of the main ways of interpreting the name that is given to Moses is to see it as communicating something central about the essence of God. Here the phrase *'ehyeh 'asher 'ehyeh* is thought of as a noun that describes God's nature. However, in contrast to this interpretation there is another way to understand this name, one that interprets it as a verb. When this name is translated as a noun it is generally rendered as "I AM WHO I AM."[64] However, if one is to approach it as a verb it can be translated as "I-shall-be-there-howsoever-I-shall-be-there."[65] By approaching it in this way the name takes on a very different characteristic: it becomes a type of name that refuses to name. God is here presented as claiming that God cannot be named at all, or rather, that God is the name we give to that which is beyond all names.

Instead of rendering God present to the understanding, this way of reading the text interprets the phrase *'ehyeh 'asher 'ehyeh* as a means of describing the nature of God's presence among us. Here God is presented neither as reducible to the status of other objects, nor as outside the world and eternally distant from it, but rather as one who is received by us without ever being directly conceived by us. Here the mystery of God is revealed as an incarnated mystery, that is, the mystery of God is revealed in the midst of God's presence. God is here being presented as saying something akin to, "Do not try to name me. My name is above all names; I am present to you beyond all names."

Here we find a different way of approaching God: here we come across the idea that God is made manifest as a happening, an event, a blessing. God is here revealed as one who is made present through the acts of love and liberation rather than through the categories of human understanding. This does not mean that we will come to an understanding of God through closely observing the actions of God. Here the text goes further: God is made known only *in* action, only *as* blessing.

In this narrative Moses expresses both the human temptation to render the source of faith into an object and the divine refusal to play along. Here we witness God as present with Moses in a way that resists the grasp of the philosophers as well as the incantations of magicians and high priests. Here we witness a presence beyond presence, a presence with and without presence. We encounter God in this narrative, not as one who is distant and thus *unknown*, nor as one object among other objects that can be rendered *known*: rather we find an expression of God as *un/known*.

God is here presented as dwelling beyond human grasp, outside human manipulation, and utterly transcendent to our categories of understanding. However, this is not a claim that God is withdrawn from the world, for this name reveals God operating as a rupture within the world. In contrast to the idea that existence relates to objects, and objects must be able to be reflected upon, Moses, and along with him the reader, is presented with a God utterly beyond objectification and yet who resides with us. Here God is presented as informing Moses that God does not exist, at least not in the way that we think of existence today.

So then, what we encounter is more than some refusal by God to be named. Here God is named as a verb. God is revealed in this narrative as a happening. God is made manifest in the faith, hope, and love that will fuel Moses' mission to set his people free.

Is this not also what we witness taking place in the story of Jacob wrestling with God? After the fight Jacob inquired after God's name. In response God says, "Why do you ask my name?" At first this appears to be a refusal to answer the question that has been asked. However, after God asks the question "Why do you ask my name?" the story informs us that God blesses him. Is it possible that this blessing was not some action unrelated to Jacob's question but rather a direct response to it? Is it possible that we are being presented here with the idea that God's name is not a description but a blessing?

Instead of rendering God present to the understanding, the stories of Jacob at the ford of Jabbok and Moses in the Midian desert hint at the radical nature of God's presence among us, a presence that cannot be made present to our understanding or experience. Here God is revealed neither as reducible to the status of other objects, nor as outside the world and distant from it, but rather as one who is *received without being conceived.*

Here the deep truth of the Judeo-Christian tradition is exposed as an intimate, life-transforming encounter with that which cannot be rendered into an object of detached contemplation and idle consideration. As was true of Jacob there are times when we wish to find out the name of the divine stranger that we wrestle with throughout our lives, when we seek to understand the one who calls us into new life, a life full of joy and peace, pain and sorrow. Yet the source with whom we wrestle is not to be approached in such a way. We are named by the source, we do not name it.

The truth of faith

So what does it mean to claim that the truth affirmed by Christianity is not a description but an event, not a fact to be grasped but an incoming to be undergone? It means that the truth affirmed by Christianity is not primarily related to some external facts such as the age of certain Gospels or the particular facts contained in them. These are interesting and important issues that should be debated and reflected upon. However, the deep truth of Christianity is not found in the acceptance of some particular historical claim. Rather, it refers to a happening testified to within the Bible that cannot be reduced to words, confined in concepts, or divulged by definitions. The truth of Christianity is not something that can be reduced to intellectual affirmations or experiential moments that can be objectified and dissected by experts.

Yet, this idea can reach our ears as an intellectual scandal. For how is it possible to think of the truth affirmed by Christianity as something that is present and yet not thought, as encountered but not able to be objectified, as there and yet absent? How can we think of faith in a way that transcends our thought, that is infinitely richer and more life-giving than mere claims to mundane facts?

In order to understand this scandal it is important to note that not everything that impacts us can be reflected upon or experienced; not everything in our world can be expressed in the realm of words and feelings. The paradigmatic example of this is life itself. Take the life of those around us: no matter how hard we look, we can never see the life of another; we merely witness the manifestation of this life in people's gestures. We can never directly experience the life of another. The physical sciences offer no more insight into the phenomenon of life than philosophy, for the sciences study physical structures, and life is not to be found under a microscope or in a test tube. Life radiates from the flesh but is not able to be reduced to the flesh: life never gives itself over to be dissected in a biology lab. In our interactions with others, we presuppose their life, we encounter their life, we undergo their life, but we never experience or understand their life as such. The presence of their life is never rendered present.

However, it is not simply the life of those around us that lies beyond the realm of our experience; at a much more radical level we cannot even experience our own life. Our own life is not something we can experience, for it is that which allows us to experience in the first place. Our life is not approached as an object in the world that can be experienced; rather it is an opening that allows us to experience objects in the world. Any deep reflection upon our own life leads to the dizzying conclusion that this life that we are, while present in the moment of reflection, is radically absent to the world of our experience.

This idea of life as beyond the realm of objectivity can be compared to our experience of light. No matter how wide we open our eyes or how hard we stare we cannot see the light that illumines our world. Just as the light in a room is not seen but rather enables us to see, so our life is not experienced but enables us to experience. Our life does not then exist like objects we encounter on a daily basis; however, it is undeniable that our own life is present to us. This can help us to understand what we mean by saying that God is not a problem to be solved but rather a mystery to participate in. For, like God, our life cannot be understood if we distance ourselves from it and treat it as an object of contemplation. Rather we must explore it indirectly, understanding that it is testified to in the midst of our engagement with the world rather than caught by treating it as an object in our world. God is no more an object in the world than our life is an object in the world. Rather, God is that which grounds our world and opens a world up to us.

Indeed, the truth affirmed by Christianity is not merely similar to the notion of life, in the sense that it is undergone rather than experienced, but rather it is that which claims to bring us life. Just as God is presented as speaking life into the formless void in Genesis, so the truth affirmed by Christianity is that which breathes life into the darkness and desolation of our own lives.

The Witness of the Jesus of the Gospels

This idea of the truth of faith as life can be witnessed in many of the teachings we find on the lips of Jesus in the Gospels, so much so that it acts as an underlying signature to all of his works. Regardless of the historical questions that can be asked of the Gospels, there is the constant claim by those who penned these works that this man Jesus brought life to those who encountered him. In addition to this we find time and time again examples of Jesus explicitly describing the truth of his message in the language of life. This is particularly the case in the Gospel of John, where we find repeated references to Jesus being life, bringing life, and offering life. From the very beginning of the Gospel, we are introduced to Jesus as emanating life (John 1:4) and from then on we repeatedly encounter the message that he offers life to those who seek it (John 3:15, 4:14, 6:33–40, 6:47–51, 8:12, 10:10, 11:25). Indeed we even find an explicit connection between truth and life in John 14:6 when we read, "I am the way and the truth and the life."

We also see this theme repeatedly arising in relation to numerous miracles and in the other writings of the New

Testament. This new life that is testified to constantly in the Bible, as our reflections show, cannot be thought of as something that one sees, touches, or even experiences. It cannot be a mere object in the world. Rather, it can be thought of only as the incoming of that which transforms all our relationships with objects in the world. *In short, it is that which fundamentally changes how we interact with the things we see, touch, and experience.*

When Jesus spoke of being "born again" he was not referring to some proposition that could be considered through logic, religious sermons, Bible reading, or through some kind reflection on religious experience; *rather he was speaking of an event that opens up a whole new world of experience.* Religious experience, in its fundamental form, is not then an experience at all but rather a counter-experience, one that transforms our mode of being in the world rather than being reduced to some strange feeling. With the incoming of this truth nothing necessarily changes in the physical world, no new object enters our horizon. But in its aftermath the person is never the same again, for everything has changed. This luminous life can never be captured, contained, or pulled apart; it is lived. This event in which nothing changes is an event so radical that nothing remains the same.

Conversion as birth

This means that the truth spoken of within the Judeo-Christian tradition transcends the mundane level of debates concerning the accuracy of certain historical claims, interesting as such debates may be. This does not in any way mean that parts of the Bible do not make historical, geographical, and archaeological assertions, but rather that the real kernel of Christianity is referring to something infinitely deeper, richer, and more esoteric than some factual claim that can be accepted or rejected without any significant change in the individual. This insight is what led the great Danish philosopher Søren Kierkegaard to speak of Christian faith as radically subjective. With this description he did not mean that the truth affirmed by Christianity is merely something made up by the individual, but rather that it is so intimately tied up with the transformation of the subject that it cannot be rendered into an object of contemplation. This truth is of such a nature that it transforms a person's subjectivity.

It is this idea of truth that we see at work in the scriptural understanding of conversion as a radical change in the subjectivity of the individual. Although conversion may be accompanied by experience, it refers to something deeper than experience, and while it may involve a radical change in one's thinking it cannot be captured in thought. Regardless of whether the event of conversion is dramatic or gradual, accompanied with tears or indifference, it transcends all of this.

Because of the utterly immanent nature of this transcendental birth, all reflection fails to grasp it. In Christianity we call the source of this conversion "God," but the moment we turn toward this source as an object, as an "it," we lose sight of that source. This can be expressed in the ambiguity found in the letters G-O-D-I-S-N-O-W-H-E-R-E. Placed together they can be read either as "GOD/IS/NOW/HERE" or as "GOD/IS/NOWHERE." One could say that these letters capture something about the view of God housed within so much of the Judeo-Christian tradition, a tradition that affirms a presence that is absent, dwelling deeply in the "now here" and yet experienced or understood as "nowhere."

For this reason it is problematic to think that people who have undergone a conversion have experienced God, while people who have not undergone this rebirth experience an absence of God. Rather, it is only the one who has undergone conversion who experiences the absence of God (the experience of God as a counter-experience). This is similar to the fact that it is only the lover who experiences the absence of the one she or he loves (i.e., experiencing the beloved as a presence that is to come). Here God is approached as the name we give to the incoming of that which opens up a new, life-giving mode of engaging with the world in all its horror and beauty.

Revelation as rupture

This idea of God as that which dwells beyond our ability to objectify, and the previous exploration of God's Word as hinted at as an inaccessible wound within, but not of, Scripture are each exposed and expressed in the Christian idea of revelation. Within the Bible we encounter revelation as the felt concealment of God. Rather than God being rendered manifest in revelation, this term can be seen to define a tight web of three interrelated features. First, a revelation worthy of the name involves *epistemological incomprehension*. In other words, part of the evidence that a revelation has occurred lies in the fact that what we have encountered cannot be understood within our currently existing intellectual structures. Second, there is *experiential bedazzlement*. Here the incoming of revelation is evidenced in a type of oversaturation in which our experience is overcome. One is overwhelmed by the incoming and short-circuited by it. Third, there is an *existential transformation*. When a revelation occurs, the person who is receiving it is never the same again.

In order to see revelation at work let us take the paradigmatic conversion of the New Testament, namely the conversion of Saul on the road to Damascus. In this famous conversion Saul is literally knocked off his horse and blinded by the incoming of revelation.[66] This event overcomes him both emotionally and intellectually, and utterly alters his entire way of interacting with the world. The result is that Saul is never the same again; taking on the name Paul, he is utterly transformed, having a total change of heart (what is called, within theology, a *metanoia*).

Rather than thinking that we are ignorant of God before God arrives on the scene, we can thus say that true ignorance of God occurs with the incoming of God. In our lives we have been exposed to so many images and ideas about God, many of which have been deeply embedded within us from childhood, that we have an abundant reservoir of understanding. Then, in the moment of revelation, the tranquility of this reservoir is disturbed. Revelation enters our world as a wound of unknowing. It ruptures our present in the guise of an eschatological "to come."

Is it not this very logic that we see expressed in the genealogy of Matthew? Here we find a human lineage for Jesus that is split into three sets of fourteen. Beginning with Abraham it charts an ancestral line to the house of David. Then it moves forward another fourteen generations to the Babylonian deportation, and finally, after another fourteen generations it brings us to Joseph, followed by Mary, and then, finally, Jesus. The result is that Jesus is solidly located within the Jewish tradition. He is presented as an intricate part of that tradition and depicted as the one that tradition has been straining toward from the very beginning. This description of an unbroken line from Abraham to Jesus is a means of showing that Jesus is perfectly placed to be the Messiah.

However, there is an immediate and obvious problem with this genealogy, for at the very end Matthew records a radical rupture in the line. At the end of the genealogy we are presented with the idea that Jesus has no blood connection with Joseph at all. Instead Matthew informs us that Jesus was conceived of Mary through the direct intervention of God. Here Jesus is placed into the genealogy, yet at the same time Jesus acts as that which causes a tear or rupture in the genealogy. The line is used to affirm the authority of Jesus, yet Jesus simultaneously acts as the rent that breaks the line. Here Matthew provides no analysis of this fissure in the genealogy; we are simply left to ponder it. Jesus does not continue the line but breaks with it. Matthew both charts the genealogical line, showing that it is important, yet clearly states that Joseph had nothing to do with the conception of Jesus, thereby simultaneously rendering the genealogy redundant.

On the one hand Matthew understands the incoming of God through Jesus as directly related to the Jewish tradition, yet on the other hand he speaks of this event as one that ruptures the tradition, that cannot be contained within it. Jesus simultaneously is inscribed within and tears apart the narrative. Here there is a respect for the ancient narrative and an affirmation of a new beginning within it, a beginning that ruptures the tradition that it respects and within which it is inscribed. Here Christianity is shown, not simply as the continuation of the Jewish tradition, but as an incoming that breaks the tradition wide open. Here we again witness the self-conscious parallactical structure of the text. The event of God is presented here as arising from, yet not contained within, the tabernacles of our traditions.

An irreligious religion

This process by which Matthew relates Jesus to the very tradition that his presence ruptures helps to expose the sense in which Christianity is structured as an irreligious religion. We can see here how the revelation of Christ forms a fissure within Judaism itself. While this has since been taken as the beginning of a new religion (Christianity), there is a sense in which Jesus is actually introducing (or re-inscribing) a wound into the already existing religion. In this sense Christianity is not that which comes after the rupture of Jesus but rather is the name that one ought to give to the rupture itself.

What we witness here is a beautiful example of the Judeo-Christian notion that when revelation takes place, with the full power of its overabundant luminosity, our religious ideas, important as they are, break open to new and vibrant possibilities. This can help us understand why Kierkegaard wrote of his distaste for people who speak of the source of faith being distant in terms of time and near in terms of understanding. For in revelation we learn that the source of our faith is near in terms of time (right here, right now, in this transformative moment), yet distant in understanding (always rupturing any of the conceptual constructs we create). This is what we have already witnessed in the Exodus encounter between Moses and God. There we do not encounter a revelation that makes God manifest, nor a revelation that places God at an absolute distance; rather, God's distance is maintained in overwhelming presence. We are presented here with God as beyond understanding and yet affirmed in a lived knowledge that cannot be reduced to propositional knowing. Here the God of the Israelites is revealed as existing on a different plane altogether from that of the Egyptian gods, who have names that can be spoken. God is known in the withdrawing of God.

The stories of Lilith in the Garden, Moses in the desert, and Jacob by the ford of Jabbok all hint at a pre-critical intimate relationship with the source of faith that existed in an unadulterated form before humans ever attempted to reify this relationship into a word. Each story informs us that the protagonist's ignorance of God was not born from an absence of God but rather amidst the presence of God. And each expresses the desire to try and name this primordial, pre-theoretical encounter. So then, instead of remaining faithful to the elusive (hyper)presence of God, each of these individuals is tempted to betray it by reducing God to a name. But God, at least when it comes to Jacob and Moses, refuses to play along, showing that fidelity to the divine (hyper)presence forever requires a readiness to betray the names we bestow upon it.

The attempt to render God present as an idea is reflected in so much of what passes as theology in the Western tradition. The result is a depiction of the theologian as a type of alchemist or wizard. For instead of being evoked *by* the mystery of faith, the theological alchemist seeks to *expose* it, while the theological wizard endeavors to *evoke* it. In this way so much theology is a means of attempting to render the ineffable as a legitimate object of inquiry rather than a circumspect discourse that limits itself to the *effect* of the ineffable upon the individual and community. In contrast to this the Christian must understand that the scriptural narrative includes a proclamation that we cannot grasp God within *any* narrative. Here God is both negated and affirmed at one and the same time, for the one we worship is revealed with the aid of religion yet cannot be constrained by it.

So, the idea that the truth affirmed by Christianity is beyond all finding out does not rest with the somewhat inane insight that we lack the minds, time scale, and data needed to make a final judgment upon some set of propositional statements, nor that being embedded within a geographical, historical, and psychological framework prevents us from forwarding some kind of totalizing Christian system. More fundamentally, the truth of faith eternally transcends any attempts at reduction to understanding and system. In this way the Christian understanding of revelation is more akin to the Eastern idea of enlightenment than to the scientific pursuit of information.

By grasping this we come face to face with a second type of faithful betrayal. In the first we saw that in order to accept the Bible we needed to reject any interpretation as final, being ready to engage in an ongoing, open-ended dialogue and discussion with it. As we come to the end of part two, we must learn that in order to approach the God of faith and the truth affirmed by Christianity, we must betray the God we grasp—for the God who brings us into a new life is never the God we grasp but always in excess of that God. The God we affirm is then, at its best, inspired by the incoming of God and born there, but it is never to be confused with God.

In the aftermath of God's happening the true worshiper attempts to paint the most beautiful pictures imaginable to reflect that happening. It is this heartfelt endeavor to paint the most refined and beautiful conceptual images that speaks of God, not the actual descriptions we create.[67] Is this not the very thing that the New Testament warns us against in 1 Timothy 6:15–16 when we read that God is the sovereign who is immortal and "lives in unapproachable light," one whom "no one has seen or can see"? Our theology then is the grand architectural conceptual cathedral we create as a worshipful response to the one who dwells in this unapproachable light, rather than a direct description.

PART 3
THE EVENT OF GOD

SEVEN

SEVEN

The Intervention of God?

Is it really God at all?

So far we have explored how the idea of God cannot be reduced to some abstract intellectual system but rather refers to a presence that cannot be rendered present, a reception that is not equivalent to conception. In this section, I want to turn our attention to the nature of this reception. If God is not to be thought of in terms of objectivity but rather as the incoming of life, then what does this mean for Christianity? For it would seem that once we affirm the idea that God lies beyond our ability to contemplate, we have to ask why we should even use the name "God" at all. Why not call this source something else entirely, or call it nothing whatsoever? In addition to this, why should one bother calling oneself a Christian in the first place? If the event of faith escapes all religious systems, then such a term would seem overly narrow and constrictive.

However, it is important to note that such thinking does not place us in any way at odds with Christianity but rather emanates directly from a deep and sustained engagement with it. Far from undermining Christianity, it could be argued that this very tradition encourages us to both understand and accept that the truth that it affirms transcends any language, culture, or religion. In short, this acknowledgment, which seems to undermine Christianity, is actually a deeply Christian insight.

The end of religion as its beginning

I t would be a mistake to think that the critique of Christianity as a religion is primarily an attack that is launched by those outside the tradition; rather, it would be better to think of it as an integral part of Christianity itself. For instance, let us consider the parable that Jesus tells as he attempts to offer people a tangible sense of the kingdom:

> What shall we say the kingdom of God is like, or what parable shall we use to describe it? It is like a mustard seed, which is the smallest of all seeds on earth. Yet when planted, it grows and becomes the largest of all garden plants, with such big branches that the birds can perch in its shade.[68]

The most common interpretation of this parable goes something like this: Jesus was claiming that the movement he instigated will continue to grow until it becomes a great institution that provides shelter for all those who seek sanctuary in it. Here Jesus is cast as the founder of Christianity, a religion (*the* religion) that will bring salvation to the world.

Yet there is another, more subversive, way of reading the above parable, one that takes us in a very different direction from the idea that Jesus is the founder of Christianity. According to the second reading, the birds of the air are not to be mistaken for a symbol of the innocent taking shelter; rather they are symbols of evil. The reason for this understanding is partly based upon the idea that such symbolism is used elsewhere within the Bible, such as when birds steal the seed of God from the earth.[69] The result is an interpretation that stands in sharp contrast to the traditional one. Here we are presented with the idea that this wonderful way of love and healing that Jesus is demonstrating will one day be reified into a vast institution that will house great evil.

This more subversive reading has also had its faithful adherents in those who would see Christ as demonstrating a way of being in the world (the way of love and healing) rather than a way of believing things about the world. These individuals would see Christianity, not as a religion at all, but rather as a critique of all religion.

Of course, those who advocate the first reading do not reject the idea that Christianity is about love and healing. Rather, the difference lies in the fact that the second approach goes much further than the claim that Christianity is *more* than a system, but rather asserts that Christianity is a *rejection* of all systems. Unlike the former reading, which sees Christianity as a worldview that can somehow be compared and contrasted with other worldviews,[70] this latter approach questions the idea that Christianity can be approached as a religious worldview at all; rather, in this approach Christianity operates within all worldviews, at least in those places where people's lives reflect love, hope, and passionate commitment to one's neighbor. While the first interpretation sees Jesus as the founder of the one true religion, the latter interpretation sees in Jesus one who would set an axe to all religion.

Initially it would seem difficult, when confronted with these alternative interpretations of the parable, to decide which offers a better description of the Church today. For, depending upon where and how we look, we can see parts of the Church that are involved with acts of great kindness in the world and other parts that have been implicated in great evil. Perhaps in light of this, we should not attempt to choose between the two options, as if one grasps the radical nature of Christ's message in isolation from the other, but rather embrace both interpretations—bringing them together in a way that opens up an approach to faith that moves beyond the limitations of each.

There is a powerful representation of this idea in the old town located in the heart of Geneva. In the main square stands St. Peter's Cathedral, an ancient building that was commandeered by Calvin as part of the Reformation. This great architectural structure stands as a powerful symbol of institutional religion. Yet, at the other end of the square, there stands a formidable statue of Jeremiah, carved, I am told, by one of Rodin's students, turning away in shame and disgust from the church. One's first reaction when confronted by these two poles is to ask which one we ought to gravitate toward, which one better captures the nature of Christianity.

Yet perhaps it is more accurate to say that the Christian is one who stands between these two images, embracing both the church and Jeremiah, manifesting elements of both priest and prophet, celebrating both the religion that began with Jesus and its overcoming. Here, in this space, Christianity finds its radical message as a religion without religion.

Christianity thus ought not be understood as either purely religious or irreligious, and the church should not be fully embraced as necessary or rejected as unnecessary. Rather, Christianity is structured as ir/religious and the church as a structure attempting to live with its un/necessary status. Christianity grounds us and yet invites us to gaze beyond its walls. As we attempt to understand our faith, we will develop ideas and practices that help us. Yet the point is that we must always be ready to critique these ideas and practices, for they are forever provisional. To display our fidelity to them we must always be ready to betray them.

As such the critique of Christianity as a religion derives from Christianity itself. Hence the statement by Karl Marx that the beginning of all critique lies in the critique of religion[71] can be seen as a profoundly religious assertion—one that is borne witness to in the lives of prophets such as Jeremiah and Amos, in Jesus, and in many of the great Christian leaders throughout history.[72] Christianity affirms an idea of truth that transcends any system, and thus the Christian is one who is, in the moment of being a Christian (i.e., standing in a particular tradition), also the one who rejects it (remembering the prophets of old who warned us about how any tradition could become idolatrous)—

betraying it as an act of deep fidelity. It is for this reason that the authentic believer can be described as a non-Christian in the Christian sense of the term.

The faith in Christ and the faith of Christ

This ir/religious drive of Christianity can be further elucidated as we acknowledge how the Christian operates amidst the tension created between the faith *of* Christ and confessing a faith *in* Christ.[73] Put differently, a Christian seeks to be embraced by the living source emanating from Jesus— that deep, living faith that existed before the existence of Christology and the various dogmas of the Church. However, flowing from this will inevitably come certain views about Jesus that, within the church, are reflected in the doctrinal affirmations developed in his aftermath.

This tension can be illustrated via an anecdote that describes a situation in which the Catholic Church protected a group of Jews from persecution by letting them take refuge in Vatican City. The problem with this arrangement was that, as time passed, some priests became concerned that the community had stayed too long. They became distressed by the situation and approached the pope with their concerns, saying, "Father, Vatican City is a Catholic refuge and a beacon of Christian light for the world. While we must help our Jewish friends, we cannot allow them to settle here." The pope was not prepared to simply ask these guests to leave, and so he asked some of his emissaries to go to the Jewish community and ask if the chief rabbi would agree to a debate. If the rabbi won, the community would be able to stay as long as they desired; however, if he lost, the community would have to pack up their possessions and move on. The chief rabbi agreed, and a date was set for the great debate. The only problem was that there was a language barrier, and both the pope and the rabbi wished to debate in private, so it was decided that the debate would be held purely with hand signals.

When the day finally arrived, the pope signaled the beginning of the debate by holding up three fingers. The rabbi immediately responded by holding up one finger. The pope hesitated and then put his hand in the air, waving it in a large circle. Again, without hesitation the rabbi pointed to the ground. Finally the pope stood up and went over to a large table upon which lay some bread and a silver chalice full of wine. Picking these up, he showed them to the rabbi with a smile. In response the rabbi reached into a bag beside him and pulled out a luscious red apple, holding it aloft, before leaving. As soon as he had left the room some priests ran up to the pope and asked who had won. The pope was visibly shocked and weakened by the debate. Shaking his head he said, "The community can stay. The rabbi had an answer for everything. First I held three fingers aloft to signify the glorious triune nature of God, but the rabbi held one finger aloft reminding me of God's wondrous unity. Then I held my hand aloft and waved it in a circle to signify that God is transcendent, inhabiting the heavenly realm, but the rabbi pointed to the ground reminding me of God's immanence in the world. Finally, I showed him the bread and wine as the body and blood of Christ, the second Adam, but my rabbi friend, second-guessing me at every point, had known to bring in an apple, reminding me of the fall and the first Adam who preceded the sacrifice of Christ."

At the same time some of the Jewish leaders rallied around the chief rabbi to hear what had happened. "Incredible," said the rabbi, "I can't believe what just happened. First he tells me that we have three days to leave, but I signal that not one of us will go. Then he says that he is going to round us all up, but I told him that we are staying rooted to the spot." Then the leaders asked, "So what happened next?" "That's the most frustrating thing of all," replied the rabbi. "Then we broke for lunch."

The reason this anecdote works is that it capitalizes on a misunderstanding generated by the contrast between a Christian doctrinal emphasis concerning faith with a more Hebraic emphasis upon the lived outworking of religious conviction in concrete existence. However, this traditional understanding makes more sense, not if we see one as a Christian approach and the other as Jewish, but rather if we see this as a tension that is opened up by and operates within the traditions themselves.

While certain beliefs are affirmed as a means of reflecting upon the faith of Jesus, these beliefs can never take the place of, or fully describe, that faith. A metaphor that may help to illustrate this relationship concerns a beautiful, bright-white dove that, one day while flying through the air, imagines how high and fast she could soar if only the air, with all its resistance, did not exist. Never did this dove realize that it was the air she cursed, with all of its restrictive forces, that allowed her to rise up in the first place. We must endeavor to understand then how the common critique that Christianity offers a particular, "narrow" stance in relation to the transcendent fails to understand that this "constrictive" location is itself a privileged opening into the transcendent. It is only by locating oneself in a narrow particular site, perceived as such, that one can gaze beyond it.

The call comes first

In short, such an approach reveals that Christianity exhibits the structure of a religion without religion. Belief thus has an important place; however, it is ultimately subordinate to the event that it points toward. The result is the idea that living within the event that is testified to in Christianity is more important than the affirmation that one is a Christian, or in other words, the event contained in the affirmation of God is more important than the belief in God.

There is an anecdote about the theologian Karl Barth that may help to clarify this idea. It is said that after a seminar one day a woman asked Barth if it was true that the serpent, spoken of in the Torah, literally spoke. In response Barth turned to her and said, "Madam, it does not matter whether or not the serpent really spoke; all that matters is what the serpent said."

Let us take this answer and apply it to the question of God. Following this logic, if someone asks us, "Do you believe that God exists?" instead of answering with a yes, no, or not sure, the properly religious response would be, "The question is not whether God exists but rather what God has said." Here the Word of God is privileged over the being of God.

In other words, philosophers can sit around debating the existence of God as a being out there, a question that is not without interest to many. However this is not, properly speaking, a religious question; it is not the kind of query that those who have been caught up in the truth of faith stake their life upon. If anything, it is the kind of question one talks about over a beer in the local pub, but not in a church. In contrast to this, the religious question could be said to relate to what God has said. This comes before any question concerning the existence of God and remains after all those discussions have run their course. Questions concerning the essence of God, the nature of sin, or the historical life of Jesus can and should be discussed. However, a faith cannot be built upon such fragile propositional foundations.

Once we add this to the insights of chapter three, namely that the Word of God is not something that communicates propositional concepts, then we will not misunderstand this privileging of the Word by thinking that it is something that enters our world as that which we can isolate, consider, and reflect upon. As we have already explored, the communication of God is such that nothing is said in the saying. Rather, a life-giving event takes place, a happening occurs, an earthquake in our being fractures us. Like the apostle Paul, we are knocked to the ground, blinded and changed by the Word.

If the call of God were something akin to an actual voice communicating ideas, then this very communication would become a blockage to God. If this voice were anything other than a happening, it could so easily be heard without being heeded, offering insight without enlightenment. We could then compare this divine call to listening to an opera in which we can be so captivated by the poetry of the words that we fail to hear the event that is contained in the opera, the event that gave birth to the opera, the event that is more important than the opera. This divorce between voice and action is evidenced in an old Italian anecdote about some soldiers who were at the front lines of a battle. These soldiers were very frightened about what lay on the other side of the bunker and, being Italian, loved the arts. Finally the general approached and shouted at the top of his voice, "Go ahead, men, attack!" But nobody moved. As the general stared in disbelief, one of the men whispered, "What a majestic voice he has."

If the truth affirmed by Christianity lay in something that people could intellectually grasp, then the truth of faith would be something that one could hold without ever hearing or following its demand. But Christianity, as a religion without religion, is too elusive to be held in this way. It does not allow for such a divorce between the hearing and the happening, for its saying does not occur in that which is said, but rather in the undergoing of an event. The divine Word, like that spoken of in Genesis, results in life being birthed in the depths of our being. In the anecdote about the Italian soldiers, we see that it was possible for them to hear the call and yet fail to heed it. However, the call of faith is one that is heard only in its transformative effect. It is a still, small voice that is heard only in being heeded.

The intervention of God

Let us approach this idea by considering the commonly held belief in an interventionist God. Such a belief is of course open to question, and anyone who has embraced Christianity will, at various times, struggle with such an idea. After all, suffering and pain are evidenced all around, and reconciling this with the idea of a loving, all-powerful God can prove extremely difficult. When we come to questioning this belief, we can find ourselves drawn toward two alternatives. On the one hand, we may come to wonder whether there is actually a God at all. We may begin to wonder how such a being could exist when one considers the dark, lifeless expanse of the universe and the fact that most human life over the majority of history has, in the words of Thomas Hobbes, been nasty, brutish, and short. On the other hand, we may conclude that God probably does exist but does not in any way get involved in what happens in life. God may be needed in order to explain the existence of the universe itself, but this cannot be conceived of as a personal, interventionist God who cares about the petty concerns of human beings.

In the modern world these are the two most logical ways to doubt the idea of an interventionist God. However, there is another way in which doubt concerning this claim can raise its head—one that becomes apparent if we are sensitive to the approach outlined above—*namely, the idea that we doubt the existence of God but we retain the belief in intervention.* Here the belief in God is not primary but rather the movement of God is. One says, "I have been touched by God in a manner that is undeniable to me. However, I am still open and free to wonder, at times, whether this God of which I speak can be explained in natural terms." Or, to put it another way, one says, "As a human being I am always haunted by doubt as to questions concerning God. However, I cannot deny that something has transformed my life and that I love the source of that transformation with all of my heart."

Is this not what we see being proclaimed in the Gospel of John when we read that once Jesus had healed a man from a debilitating blindness, some of his friends brought him before the Pharisees. Here, when the man was asked whether or not he thought Jesus was a sinner, the man simply replies, "Whether he is a sinner or not, I don't know. One thing I do know. I was blind but now I see!"[74] Here we witness doubt concerning the status of Jesus but an absolute affirmation of the intervention itself. For Christians it is a happening, an event, that we affirm and respond to, regardless of the ebbs and flows of our abstract theological reflections concerning the source and nature of this happening.

All this may sound like the affirmation of doubt above all else.[75] However, nothing could be farther from the truth. Yes, doubt is affirmed in this perspective, and yes, it is welcomed and even celebrated rather than fought and repressed. However, in this reading, doubt comes in the aftermath of a happening that is itself indubitable. As we have already noted, whenever one reduces the truth affirmed in Christianity to the idea of factual claims, then doubt becomes a negative and corrosive force to be attacked. However, here doubt is embraced as a deeply positive phenomenon and is given its proper place, not as that which strikes up against the truth of faith *but as the natural outworking of this truth*. That is why doubt is intimately tied up with faith, because the deep truth of faith gives birth to doubt. It is not doubt that lies at the center here, as it does in the modern thought of Descartes, but rather a form of certainty. This is not, however, the epistemological certainty so loved by Enlightenment-influenced Christians. It is the certainty that something has happened, that a Word has taken root in our being and brought overabundant life, a certainty testified to in a renewed existence that gives rise to doubt regarding its source.

The affirmation of an intervention amidst all our doubt and uncertainty concerning its source thus represents the Christian idea that we have been marked by a life-giving event that invites us to passionately respond with our entire being. It is out of this that a deep and sustained questioning arises.

EIGHT

EIGHT

The Miracle of Christian Faith

The Event of Christianity as miracle

So far we have explored how the truth that is affirmed by Christ is nothing less than an unfathomable life-giving event. We have also reflected upon the idea that God, as expressed within the Judeo-Christian tradition, cannot be distinguished from this event. Now we will turn our attention to its nature as miracle.

Unlike the common view that would split God into the distinct categories of being, revelation, and event, the approach that we have been developing here leads to the claim that these cannot be separated. Instead, from our human perspective, they ought to be approached as exhibiting a type of Trinitarian structure whereby each is inextricably bound up with the others and affirms one and the same fundamental reality. The three are one, operating with a minimal difference, that is, a difference within the one rather than a difference that would render it into three. We misunderstand the truth of faith if we think that the nature, revelation, and event of God can be torn apart from each other and compartmentalized in isolation from one another.

Each of these is merely a different way of bringing to mind, describing, exploring, or referring to the same reality in a different register. On the lips of the believer words such as *God*, *revelation*, and *rebirth* are responses to the occurrence of an intervention, a miracle that has taken place. When Pascal wrote of the heart as having reasons that reason does not know, he was referring to a type of knowledge that is foreign to the academic disciplines and different from the type of knowledge we seek in daily life. He was referring to the knowledge of a transformation that could never be placed into words or experience and thus could never be objectified, dissected, and distanced from us.

Christian faith teaches us, if we are sensitive and able to be taught, that the seemingly opposite and opposed realms of radical doubt and absolute certainty are reconciled in a knowing beyond knowledge. There is no doubt for the believer that God dwells with us (as an event), yet there is a deep uncertainty about who, what, or even if God is (as a being). As we saw in the last chapter, the Christian is one who affirms the intervention while understanding that there will always be questions as to the source of that intervention. God, the revelation of God, and the event of God all, at their most luminous, are ways of referring to and responding to a miracle.

Deeper than magic and reason

Discussion and debates concerning the idea of miracles have generally revolved around issues to do with whether or not it is possible for events to occur that suspend or break the laws of nature. Debates have taken place concerning whether the present, future, and even the past can be altered by supernatural intervention. In addition to these questions there are a host of others connected to issues such as whether what we think is a miracle may actually be the occurrence of a natural event that we do not yet understand, whether we are ever justified in claiming to have witnessed a miracle, and what would even count as one. Indeed, there are even people who wonder whether some of the latest scientific theories concerning quantum mechanics lend credibility to, or take it away from, the possibility of a supernatural intervention. While such debates are interesting and find a happy home in undergraduate philosophy classes, these discussions can actually obscure the very thing that they are attempting to illuminate. For the Christian idea of the miraculous delves much deeper than such debates.

This does not mean that one must reject the idea of physical transformations any more than it means that one ought to embrace them. It no more means that one ought to stop praying for the sick any more than it is a call to do so. Both those reading this book who regularly engage in praying for physical healing and those who do not believe in such occurrences will find no support for their positions within these pages, for in order to get to the heart of what a miracle is we must move beyond these discussions. The miracle that Christianity affirms is too precious to be *reduced* to such a level.

There are no doubt a host of strange occurrences that take place in the world, occurrences that are often given the name "miracle." Yet the whole idea of a miracle as that which suspends or breaks the laws of nature is not only legitimately interrogated by academics but also undermined by the works of magicians, and mired by the unscrupulous acts of religious charlatans. As such, even if one deeply believes in the possibility and actuality of events of this nature, one must also acknowledge that such a position is debatable—not just in the absence of witnessing some extraordinary event but even in the presence of one.

It would be dishonest of the believer not to acknowledge that there are other valid explanations for seemingly extraordinary events that may even provide more intellectually satisfying answers. Such miracles are thus open to legitimate doubt, not only for those who have not witnessed or attempted to evoke such extraordinary events but also for those who have. It is only honest for one who prays for the sick to understand that there may be other explanations for what is taking place than the supernatural one. This does not in any way take away from the practice itself, but simply acknowledges our intellectual finitude and demonstrates openness to other perspectives.

In contrast to the above debates there is a sense in which the miracle of Christianity takes place at a level that is indubitable, at least for the person who has undergone it. This idea of miracle, as we shall see, is a full-blooded one that bears witness to an earth-shattering event that can transform the present, future, and even the past. In this event, everything is changed, and even the old is made new. However, in order to approach this miracle it is important for us to bracket out the above debates, debates that can so often eclipse the supernatural moment that Christianity affirms. Indeed we can witness this desire to avoid allowing physical healings to get in the way of the true miracle in the Gospels themselves when Jesus is presented as healing people and then, in stark contrast to what we would expect, asks them to keep the healing secret. For instance, in the Gospel of Luke we read this:

> While Jesus was in one of the towns, a man came along who was covered with leprosy. When he saw Jesus, he fell with his face to the ground and begged him, "Lord, if you are willing, you can make me clean."
>
> Jesus reached out his hand and touched the man. "I am willing," he said. "Be clean!" And immediately the leprosy left him.
>
> Then Jesus ordered him, "Don't tell anyone, but go, show yourself to the priest and offer the sacrifices that Moses commanded for your cleansing, as a testimony to them."[76]

It was as if Jesus was worried that such healings could so easily become a barrier to understanding the central miracle of the Christian faith, that some outward sign inspiring awe and devotion would stand in for the real thing.

This idea is beautifully illustrated in the Hasidic story in which the rabbi of Gur, during the Second World War, was invited to advise Winston Churchill about how to ensure the downfall of Germany. The story goes that this great rabbi looked at Churchill and solemnly said, "Prime Minister, there are two ways in which this could happen. The natural and the supernatural. The natural solution would involve a million angels with flaming swords descending upon Germany. The supernatural would involve a million Englishmen parachuting down from the sky." The story famously ends with the line that, being a rationalist, Churchill first opted for the natural solution.

The key to understanding this enigmatic message is to understand that if a million angels with flaming swords descended upon Germany, then this would be an event that took place in the natural realm. In other words these angels would act like other objects in the world; they would be seen, heard, and experienced. These angels, if they showed up as the rabbi described, would inhabit space and time like any other object and so, while unlike other objects that we encounter in the world, would still be objects.

In contrast, the rabbi speaks of a supernatural response to the Nazi war machine, namely a million British soldiers descending from the sky in parachutes. But what is it about this response that is supernatural in contrast to the image of angels descending from the heavens? Here one could say that the rabbi is hinting at a deep change in the hearts of the British that would precipitate such a drastic response. This change, for the rabbi, would be deeply supernatural in the sense that the change itself would not be something that could be captured in a laboratory or measured by reference to some purely utilitarian calculation (otherwise it would be a natural phenomenon). Unlike the descent of warrior angels, this change would not lend itself to be approached as a natural object to be reflected upon; it would not be made manifest to the senses like the angels with their flaming swords.

The point is not to exclude the idea that miracles can involve awe-inspiring, breathtaking spectacles, but rather to point out that if the event is purely spectacular, involving no real change in the core of one's being, then it is nothing more than a spectacle. Physical changes are natural insomuch as they take place in the natural realm. Our medical technology is constantly improving and is able to heal in ways that would have seemed magical only a hundred or two hundred years ago. Vital as such healing is in today's world, such a focus can eclipse what Christianity affirms as the true miracle. It is not something natural (although it will manifest itself in the natural world) but something supernatural. It does not register as an object that can be recorded and beamed around the world on some religious cable channel, or witnessed at a local charismatic healing service. A miracle worth its salt takes place in the world but is not of it. A miracle worthy of the name is so radical that while in the physical world nothing may change, in the one who has been touched by it nothing remains the same.

Consider the words of Jesus after we read that he has caused a fig tree to wither away just by speaking to it in

Matthew 21. In response to this his disciples are amazed and say, "How did the fig tree wither so quickly?" Jesus is recorded as replying, "Truly I tell you, if you have faith and do not doubt, not only can you do what was done to the fig tree, but also you can say to this mountain, 'Go, throw yourself into the sea,' and it will be done."[77]

On the surface this claim seems utterly insane. Does Jesus really mean that one could, through faith, lift a mountain and place it into the sea? Can faith really evoke a miracle that will irrevocably change an entire landscape? Yet at a fundamental level this is precisely what a miracle does in fact do. A miracle is signaled by the fact that the entire landscape of our being is transformed and transfigured. For when a miracle takes place, everything changes in the life of the individual—not only the present and the future, but also the past. Let us consider one such miracle, the act of forgiveness. When one forgives nothing changes in the world; everything continues as normal as if nothing had happened. Yet, in another sense something of fundamental significance has taken place.

Those who forgive find themselves interacting with the present in a totally different way and experience liberation from the past. The past is not forgotten; one cannot, and should not, forget great injustices. Rather, in forgiveness the past is remembered, but remembered differently, held differently, recalled differently. Nothing in the past has changed, yet it seems like a different past; the situation remains but has lost its burdensome weight. In this act of forgiveness we are freed from the past—a freedom that changes the whole trajectory of a person's life, opening up new possibilities and opportunities. Forgiveness, love, and hope are all miraculous in the supernatural sense that the rabbi of Gur was hinting at. In the language we have been using here, the miracle is not something that can be judged by the conceptual framework used in scientific research, for it does not dwell there or manifest itself directly in that exterior space.

Is this not what we see expressed in Matthew 9 when we read that a man who was paralyzed met Jesus? In contrast to what we would expect, Jesus turns to him and performs the true miracle, saying to the man, "Take heart, son; your sins are forgiven." The teachers of the law understood what was happening here—or at least they understood what Jesus was claiming to be doing—and they said to themselves, "This fellow is blaspheming!" In response to this we read:

> Knowing their thoughts, Jesus said, "Why do you entertain evil thoughts in your hearts? Which is easier: to say, 'Your sins are forgiven,' or to say, 'Get up and walk'? But I want you to know that the Son of Man has authority on earth to forgive sins." So he said to the paralyzed man, "Get up, take your mat and go home." Then the man got up and went home. When the crowd saw this, they were filled with awe; and they praised God, who had given such authority to human beings.[78]

This text is a beautiful expression of the miracle—that which transforms the core of our being, revolutionizing our interior world. The actual physical healing here is nothing more than a signpost to the real miracle. In order to understand this let us consider the following parable, inspired by a story in the Gospels.

After Jesus descended from the Mount of Olives he came across a man who had been blind from birth. And his disciples asked him, "Rabbi, who sinned, this man or his parents, that he was born blind?"

Jesus answered, "It was not that this man sinned, or his parents, but that the works of God might be displayed in him. We must carry out the works of him who sent me while it is day, for night is approaching, when no one can work. As long as I am in the world, I am the light of the world." Having said these things, he spat on the ground and made mud with the saliva. Then he anointed the man's eyes with the mud and said to him, "My friend, go, wash in the pool of Siloam." So the man went and washed and returned in jubilation, shouting, "I can see."

The neighbors and those who knew him as a beggar began to grumble saying, "Has this man lost his mind? for he was born blind." Some said, "It is he." Others said, "No, but he is like him." In response the old man kept repeating, "I am the man. Jesus anointed my eyes and said, 'Go to Siloam and wash.' So I went and washed, and now I can see everything."

To ascertain what had happened to this man since his meeting with Jesus, they brought him to the Pharisees.

"Give glory to God," they said. "We know that this man is a sinner." But the old man answered, "Whether or not he is a sinner I do not know. One thing I do know, that though I was blind, now I see."

But the Pharisees began to laugh. "Old man, meeting Jesus has caused you to lose your mind. You had to be carried into this room by friends, you still stumble and fall like a fool. You are still as blind today as the day you were born."

"That may be true," replied the old man with a long, deep smile. "As I have told you before, all I know is that yesterday I was blind but today, today I can see."[79]

Beyond believe, behave, belong

B ecause a miracle takes place at a radically subjective level that cannot be objectified or analyzed, it is not, strictly speaking, something that is believed in. Rather it is lived. Indeed it can easily be lived and not believed in. The evidence of such a miracle is in the way in which it transforms the individual's inner world, changing the entire trajectory of that person's life in a positive, healing way. How one names this miracle, or even if one wishes to baptize it with any name, is irrelevant. What matters is the occurrence. It is this miracle that the church is there to affirm by engaging in creative acts of remembrance concerning this immemorial event. However, instead of these acts of humble remembrance, much of the church has emphasized the importance of what we think. So often we find an emphasis on *belief*, followed by *behavior*, that then leads into *belonging*. For instance, if a Christian is sharing his or her faith, the discussion will likely concern a set of beliefs that one is asked to accept—beliefs that will often include the existence of God, the deity of Christ, the existence of sin, and the atoning sacrifice of Jesus. If these are accepted then the individual will be asked to engage in a certain behavior, that is, to pray, repent, and join the local church. Then, once this has taken place, that individual will be welcomed into the Christian community, being invited to get involved in the life of the church.

This approach works with the underlying idea that belief is of prime importance in Christianity, followed by behavior, followed by belonging. In contrast to this let us briefly consider the birth of an infant. When a child enters the world she does not begin with a system of beliefs that must be accepted before she belongs to the family. The infant, in a healthy environment, begins her life with absolute, unconditional acceptance. The infant belongs to the family as the family now belongs to the infant. As the child grows she gradually learns to engage in the various rituals in which the family engages. These will include times when the family members eat together, play together, relax together, and so on. Then the child will begin to form a set of beliefs about the world into which she is already embedded. These will generally begin by mimicking the beliefs of the parents. Then these beliefs will likely come into conflict with those of the parents, as she attempts to wrestle with the world for herself and test limits. And finally she will often come into some equitable relationship with the parents' beliefs, agreeing with some and disagreeing with others. Within a healthy, loving family each of these stages will be welcomed and allowed room to breathe.

This approach thus places belonging first, followed by behavior, followed last and least, by belief. This model is what we find in operation within a broadly Hebraic approach to faith, an approach that emphasizes belonging to the community and engaging in the shared rituals of that community. When it comes to our beliefs, that is, to theoretical reflection upon our embedded existence, there is an acknowledgment that we will often think and rethink these at various times in our lives. What is important is that, regardless of the doubts and beliefs we have, we know that we have a vital place in the community and are encouraged to remain involved in the traditions—traditions that, at their best, provide ample space for doubt, ambiguity, and uncertainty.

Is this not the wisdom that is contained in the Jewish parable that speaks of a heated debate taking place in a park between two old and learned rabbis? The conversation in question revolves around a particularly complex and obscure verse in the Torah. It is not the first time that these two intellectual giants have crossed swords over this verse; in fact they have debated it for years, sometimes changing their opinions but never finding a consensus. God is, of course, known to have the patience of a saint, but even God begins to tire of the endless discussion. So finally God decides to visit the two men and tell them once and for all what the parable means. God reaches down, pulls the clouds apart, and begins to speak: "You have been debating this verse

endlessly for years; I will now tell you what it means. . . . "
But before God can continue, the two rabbis look up and
say, in a rare moment of unity, "Who are you to tell us what
the verse means? You have given us the words, now leave us
in peace to wrestle with it."

In this parable we are reminded that a religious approach
to the text is not one in which we attempt to find out its
definitive meaning, but rather where we wrestle with it and
are transformed by it. The parable tells us not that a God's-
eye view is impossible, but rather that even if it were possible
it would not be wanted. Why? Because a God's-eye view of
the truth would not be the truth. We can thus say that any
interpretation of a verse that is given to us by God is not a
true interpretation of the verse and must be rejected as such.
For the problem resides not in having an interpretation but
rather in the place that we give to our interpretation. No
matter how wonderful our interpretation is, if it occupies an
authoritative place then it undermines its own status.

For the rabbis in this story the truth of the verses is not
discovered after some long, drawn-out process of debate
and discussion, but rather is evidenced within the process of
debate and discussion itself. The truth is negatively testified
to in the commitment to a constant unraveling and re-sowing
of our ideas in relationship with the text—an approach that
emphasizes the need for relationship (they are friends),
shared rituals (they are both rabbis), and the place of diverse
views (they disagree with each other).

We see this approach fleshed out in the life of Jesus
when he calls the disciples. In the Gospels we read that the

disciples are called to leave their past behind and live in close community with Jesus. It is likely that they know very little about this man, beyond perhaps that he is a subversive rabbi. Once they are part of this intimate gathering, the disciples begin to engage in shared practices. Then, finally, near the end of the ministry of Jesus, some of the disciples appear to begin to develop beliefs about who they think Jesus is. Here we witness an emphasis upon belonging, followed by behavior, followed last and least by belief. Indeed, what is interesting is Jesus' reaction when some of the disciples begin to form some beliefs that we would recognize today as a primitive form of Christology. In the Gospel of Matthew we read this:

When Jesus came to the region of Caesarea Philippi, he asked his disciples, "Who do people say the Son of Man is?"

They replied, "Some say John the Baptist; others say Elijah; and still others, Jeremiah or one of the prophets."

"But what about you?" he asked. "Who do you say I am?"

Simon Peter answered, "You are the Messiah, the Son of the living God."

Jesus replied, "Blessed are you, Simon son of Jonah, for this was not revealed to you by flesh and blood, but by my Father in heaven. And I tell you that you are Peter, and on this rock I will build my church, and the gates of death will not overcome it. I will give you the keys of the kingdom of heaven; whatever you bind on earth will be bound in heaven, and whatever you loose on earth will be loosed in heaven." *Then he ordered his disciples not to tell anyone that he was the Messiah.*[80]

It is the last line that is of particular interest. In contrast to those who wish to shout from every rooftop the belief that Jesus is the Messiah, Jesus is presented as wishing to keep this a secret—almost as if such a belief might get in the way of the good news itself.

It is such an idea that Pascal understood as he worked on his unfinished book *Pensées*. Pascal is known best for an argument that has been named Pascal's Wager. He is famous for arguing that in life one must live as though there is an ultimate personal source called God or that there is not. One cannot sit on the fence on this issue, because our decision is evidenced in our life rather than in some verbal declaration. Whether or not I say that I believe in God, the evidence of my belief is shown in whether I live as though there is a God or not. So Pascal asked whether it would be more reasonable to act as though God does not exist or to live as though God does exist, considering one has to wager one's life anyway. He then went on to argue that it would be more reasonable to bet that God does exist and live accordingly, rather than the other way around. The reason for this relates to the fact that the consequences of making this bet and being right could be very considerable, while the consequences of making this bet and being wrong would seem pretty insignificant. In contrast, betting that God does not exist significantly reduces the chances of gaining the possible pleasure that would result in betting that God does exist and being right. This is a rather simplified and concise rendering of the argument, and there are a number of legitimate problems with it. However, what is often missed when the wager is being dissected in philosophy class is the underlying idea that provoked Pascal to forge it in the first place. For the argument is very different from those that had been offered before, arguments that attempted to prove that belief in God is reasonable because of certain evidence or because of the principles of logic.

While Pascal believed that the evidence of creation and the human psyche point toward the reasonableness of Christianity, he understood that this is not relevant. What is important is that people join the religious community and engage in the rituals. This acting as if it were true was not, for Pascal, authentic Christianity, and it did not guarantee that the miracle of faith would take place. But he reasoned that it was the best place to invite this miracle. Thus he was simply attempting to construct an argument that would convince his friends, many of whom were gamblers and would have thus been intrigued by the idea of a wager—to enter into a faith community and engage in the various activities.

If one were to think of this argument in relation to the idea of love, Pascal was in effect saying that if someone does not believe in love the best approach is not to engage in some abstract debate about the subject matter but rather to convince the person to wager that love does exist and to engage in the activities that those who believe in love engage in. While this does not guarantee that one will find love, it would seem like the best place to look for it.

Communities that embrace the miracle

U p to now I have attempted to argue that the truth attested to by Christian faith is not something that we can distance ourselves from and reduce to the realm of physical objects, but rather is nothing less than the undergoing of what has been called, within the Christian tradition, a miracle. This miracle, however we understand it, is analogous to a rebirth or new life in which we are radically transformed so that our relationship to the past, present, and future is no longer the same. This miracle signals the transfiguration of our entire being. It refers to a world-shattering transformation that is hinted at it in words such as *love*, *forgiveness*, *hope*, and *faith*. The result is a truth that is both undeniable to the one who undergoes it and yet is open to doubt. For one can simultaneously question the source of this miracle while embracing it, being nourished by it and living in the light of it. Indeed, one can deny the miracle or be oblivious to it and still testify to it via one's life.

What we find within the Christian tradition is a beautiful way of remembering, embracing, being nourished by, and living in the light of this miracle despite all the legitimate concerns and doubts we may have concerning it. For Christianity, at its best, offers us a community of people who have likewise been knowingly marked by the miracle and who wish to celebrate it through shared rituals such as prayer, meditation, fasting, liturgy, serving the poor, fighting injustice, and so on.

Instead of forming churches that emphasize belief before behavior and behavior before belonging, there is a vast space within the tradition to form communities that celebrate belonging to one another in the undergoing and aftermath of the miracle, a belonging that manifests itself in communally agreed rituals, creeds, and activities. In the midst of all this these communities can also encourage lively, heated, and respectful discussions concerning the nature and form of belief.

When thinking through issues to do with morality, religion, the world, and social action, people can introduce and employ the richest thoughts of the various intellectual disciplines, because the truth that Christianity affirms does not impact these discussions in terms of content but rather in terms of approach, demanding that the conclusions we come to bring liberation and healing.

NINE

NINE

Forging Faith Communities With/out God

Faith with (mis)deeds

Christianity, as we have been endeavoring to explore, exhibits a somewhat disconcerting vertigo-inducing rupture at its very core, a divine rupture that gives it the form of a religion without religion that asks us to betray our faith tradition precisely so as to affirm it in the deepest and most radical manner. In order to express the idea of religion without religion in a concrete way let us consider the following parable:

There was once a fiery preacher who possessed a powerful gift. Far from encouraging people's religious beliefs, he found that from an early age, when he prayed for people the result would be the individual's loss of all religious convictions. When he prayed for people he found that they would often walk away having lost all of their religious beliefs, beliefs about the prophets, the sacred Scriptures, and even God. Since this was the case he would, as you might expect, rarely pray for others and instead would limit himself to sermons.

However one day, while traveling across the country, he found himself in conversation with a businessman who happened to be going in the same direction. This businessman was very wealthy, having made his money in the world of international banking. The conversation had begun because the businessman possessed a deep faith and had noticed the preacher reading from the Bible. Because of this he introduced himself and they began to talk. As they chatted together, the rich man told the preacher all about his faith in God and his love of Christ. It turned out that although he worked hard in his work he was not really interested in worldly goods.

"The world of business is a cold one," he confided to the preacher, "and in my line of work there are situations in which I find myself that challenge my Christian convictions. But when confronted by such situations, I try, as much as possible, to remain true to my faith. Indeed, it is my faith that stops me from getting too caught up in that heartless world of work, reminding me that I am really a man of God."

After listening carefully to the businessman's story, the preacher responded by asking if he could pray for him. The young man readily agreed, not knowing what he was letting himself in for. And sure enough, after the preacher had said his simple prayer, the businessman opened his eyes in astonishment.

"What a fool I have been for all these years," said the businessman. "There is no God above who is looking out for me, there are no sacred texts to guide me, there is no spirit to inspire me."

As they parted company the businessman, still confused by what had taken place, returned home with one less item than he had left with. But now that he no longer had any religious beliefs to make him question his work and hold it lightly, he was no longer able to continue with it. Faced with the fact that he was now just a hard-nosed businessman working in a corrupt system, he began to despise himself. And so, shortly after his meeting with the preacher, he gave up his line of work completely, gave the money he had accumulated to the poor, and started to use his considerable expertise in helping a local charity. One day, years later, he happened upon the preacher again while he was walking through town. The man ran up to him, fell at his feet, and began to cry. After a few moments he looked up at the preacher and said, "Thank you for helping me to discover my faith."

The key to understanding this parable lies in grasping how one's very religious convictions can actually fuel actions that would stand opposed to them. In the above example we can imagine the businessman thinking that his faith in Christ and his involvement in a local church are what encourages him to pose certain ethical questions about the industry he works in, questions about the type of investments his bank backs, the damage of debilitating international interest rates, and the greed that fuels so many of the decisions that the bank makes on a daily basis.

He thinks that it is his faith that pushes him to influence banking decisions in a manner that includes the consideration of moral issues. Although he is a tough and committed businessman who is making a great deal of money, he knows deep in his heart that he is a Christian who does not place his true value on earthly treasures. Indeed, his attempts to influence the bank in ethical ways hint at this deep truth: namely, that he does not take the world of making money and business success too seriously. It is what he does in order to provide for his family and the local church, but it is not who he is.

However, in contrast to this commonsense view of the situation, let us offer a different interpretation. In contrast to the idea that the man's faith is the deep inner truth that prevents him from fully engaging in a heartless capitalistic drive for wealth, one could say that it is precisely his faith in God that enables him to be a hard-nosed business man in the first place. While slightly moderating his drive for financial success at any cost, his supposedly true inner identity simply acts as the fuel that powers his work by allowing him to escape from facing up to the reality of his actions. In Christianity as a religion without religion one cannot make this distinction between one's actions and one's beliefs.

There are very few of us who would want to knowingly dedicate our lives to the selfish pursuit of making money at the expense of others, yet it would seem that so many of us do in fact work in such environments (in businesses that make use of child labor or that cause significant environmental damage). What if these types of destructive

businesses run efficiently precisely because most of us who
are involved, when asked, will voice concerns and even some
guilt about what we do? What if, over a drink, we confide
that we are really people with deep ethical and/or religious
convictions who have moral dilemmas about our work and
are attempting, in small but important ways, to address
these problems. While we may think that these deep ethical
and religious identities are the deep truth of our being that
helps us to undermine the immoral aspects of our activities,
perhaps these very identities are the fantasy that allows us to
engage in the activities we really desire.

In the above parable the "deep truth" of the businessman's
inner life (that he has faith in God and his family) is
actually a pragmatic fantasy that enables him to engage in
making money at other people's expense. When his faith is
removed and he looks at himself as he really is, he can no
longer embrace his occupation.

Another way in which we can see this play out concerns
various forms of political protest. We can so easily make
claims concerning the need to end child labor or look after
the environment, and yet we continue to buy the products that
employ child labor or damage the eco-system. Our religious
or political ideology here functions as that which allows
us to continue living in the way to which we have become
accustomed with a minimum of guilt. The last thing we really
want is to get what we are asking for, because this would cost
us so much in terms of how we live. We do not want to sacrifice
our comfortable lives, yet we find it hard to acknowledge that
distasteful truth, and so we engage in forms of protest that

enable us to blame another (the government, big business) while enjoying the benefits that such a corrupt system offers us. It is a little like employees talking about their manager behind her back while at the same time working hard, coming in on time, and seeking approval. The backbiting that goes on in the office is not, contrary to expectation, something that undermines the manager. If anything, it is the very valve that enables the manager to keep the employees from taking their grievances further.

From the above examples we can begin to see how the affirmation of Christianity as a religious system can allow us to think of our identity as somehow not directly implicated in our activity. However, in addition to this, religious belief systems can also directly encourage the behavior they seem to condemn. In order to understand this aspect of religious conviction let us imagine a child being told that under no circumstances is she to go into a certain cupboard and open a particular tin. It is this very prohibition that fuels the desire to engage in this activity. Yet this happens in such a way that the child experiences the prohibition as an obstacle. So the prohibition actually acts as a type of disavowed command. Or alternatively, if someone grows up in an environment in which a certain lifestyle is strongly endorsed over and against another, it is only natural that the individual will be intrigued by what is prohibited and be captivated by its pull. The power of the prohibition does not lie in whether it is correct or not but rather in its disavowed command. Hence religious and political convictions can act as the very thing that fuels the prohibited action.

Is this not what Paul intimately understood when he wrote that the law and sin are interconnected, that is, that religious prohibitions generate the very activity they attempt to abolish? And is not the radical message of Paul, a message that takes Jesus to be instigating a way out of this dichotomy, a way that emphasizes love as that which enables us to transcend our enslavement to the law and its obverse—sin? Paul understood that the law, while manifested as the obstacle to sin, secretly provided it with oxygen. So then, strange as it may first sound, religious convictions can thus provide an implicit command to act in a way that they explicitly reject.[81]

A system against systems

We need then to rediscover Christianity as a religion without religion that focuses upon the miracle of faith as that which transforms our subjectivity to such an extent that we do not need the law (which causes us to move toward sin), but which overcomes the law with love. For love fulfils the law by transcending it. Here everything is permissible even though not everything is beneficial.[82]

This idea of Christianity, that of a religion without religion, is made manifest in its own unique type of (anti)system. An ideological system is traditionally composed of a set of beliefs that attempt to reveal the way life ought to be lived. The problem with such systems, however, is that when they become powerful they become destructive, for in the affirmation of every system there are those who stand outside it and who are excluded from it. Political and religious systems implicitly or explicitly sacrifice individuals whose beliefs and actions do not fit with the ideology.

Christianity, conceived of as a system, begins with a religious or political mode of thinking and then seeks to impose it upon the world. Here a strong Platonic influence is at work whereby we mold the particular (the individual) into the Universal (the idea), and if the individual can't—or won't—be molded, then he or she is rejected.[83] For instance, if a certain lifestyle is perceived to be wrong within the system's framework, the individual in question will be asked to change or leave. The disavowed obverse of "all humans are part of my family" is then, "if you will not be part of my family you are not human."

Various systems or worldviews fight for power and authority. Yet Christianity, as a religion without religion, offers a radically different approach. Christ opens up the idea of a system that seeks always to find those who are excluded from the system that is in power. The Christian "worldview" is thus manifested as always seeking out those who have been rejected from the worldviews that have authority. The way this works itself out in practice is that whatever political or religious idea is dominating the society at any given time, Christianity seeks out those who are excluded by it, the one sheep who is not in the pen, the one coin not in the purse, those who have not been invited to the party, the nobodies, the nothings.[84] The Christian "system" can thus never take power for, by definition, it is always that which stands against power, seeking to identify with the powerless and the voiceless. It is a system in the sense that it systematically seeks out those who do not fit into the system offered up by the currently prevailing political and religious authorities.

What we see being worked out within Christianity can thus be said to be a prejudice toward those who are excluded and marginalized, those who are oppressed by our religious and political systems. This means that every time a "Christian" system is created, the Christian is the one who seeks out those who are excluded from it. Christianity, as a religion without religion, affirms a system that undermines every system of power by seeking those who are oppressed. The Christian critique is not then directed at the people in power so much as at the place of power itself. When a system of thought, however great, is given authority over all, it becomes oppressive and undermines its own liberative elements. The point then is not to find the "right" way of thinking and then give it a place of power and influence, but rather to question the place of power and influence itself. Is this not what we learn from the following biblical insight?

> For our struggle is not against flesh and blood, but against the rulers, against the authorities, against the powers of this dark world and against the spiritual forces of evil in the heavenly realms.[85]

Here we see that a radical Christianity is not about overthrowing the one who is in authority (who is flesh and blood) but rather about overthrowing the place of authority itself (e.g., instead of overthrowing the king we overthrow the whole idea of a king). Here the scandal of Christianity is that it offers a view of God, not as a master, but as a servant. In the Gospels we learn of God as one who comes in weakness to overthrow the religious powers. We should then always be sensitive to the subtle ways that our own thinking can act as a power that excludes and oppresses. Once we identify those whom we exclude, then we can seek them out and allow them to subvert our own ideas. This movement is expressed beautifully in the following parable written by Philip Harrison:

The other day I had a dream. I dreamed I arrived at the gates of heaven, heavy-shut, pure oak, bevelled and crafted, glinting sharp in the sunlight. St. Peter stood to greet me; the big man wore brown, smile set deep against his ruddy cheeks.

"You're here," he said.

"I am," I said.

"Great to see you—been expecting you," he smiled. "Come on in."

He pushed gently against the huge door; it swung silently, creakless. I took a couple of steps forward until, at the threshold, one more step up and in, I realized I wasn't alone. My friends had joined me, but they hovered behind, silently, looking on. None spoke. I realized only I could speak. I looked at them; some were Christians, some Hindus, some Buddhists, some Muslims, some Jews, some atheists. Some God knows what. I stopped, paused. A hesitant St. Peter looked at me, patiently, expectantly.

"What about these guys?" I asked him. "My friends. Can they come?"

"Well, Phil," he replied, soft in the still air, "you know the rules. I'm sorry, but that's the way things are. Only the right ones."

I looked at him. He seemed genuinely pained by his answer. I stood, considering. What should I do? I thought about my reference points, and thought about Jesus, the bastard, the outsider, the unacceptable, the drunkard, the fool, the heretic, the criminal, and I knew exactly where I belonged.

"I'll just stay here then too," I said, taking my one foot out of heaven. And I'll tell you, I'd swear I saw something like a grin break across St. Peter's face, and a voice from inside whispered, "At last."[86]

The point that is being made here is that Christianity, as a religion without religion, always resists being implicated in the dominant ideological systems within society by seeking to stand with those who dwell outside of them. As religion without religion Christianity's ir/religious expression cannot be reduced to a tightly held worldview without being effaced, for it is expressed fundamentally in the texture of one's life particularly in relation to the poor and oppressed. Is this not the deep insight expressed in James 2:26 when we read that faith without deeds is dead?

Transformance art

So how does this faithful betrayal work itself out in practice? How can we construct an architectural space that (1) challenges this temptation to reduce the truth affirmed by Christianity to an oppressive religious system and (2) simultaneously provides room for that truth to breathe?

By attacking the constant desire to reduce Christianity to a religious system, there is a real need for Christians to provide spaces in which religious beliefs are exposed as, at best, secondary to the deep miracle affirmed by Christianity, and, at worst, a fantasy that betrays a total absence of the miracle. Once this is understood and people are invited to begin to deconstruct their religious systems, individuals will either be brought to a deeper understanding and appreciation of their faith or they may find that they never really had faith in the first place. In the former case the deconstruction will enable the individual to delve deeper into an appreciation of his or her faith, while in the latter the individual will leave such things behind. Both of these are preferable to either mistaking the true miracle of faith for a system of thought or of using that system as a way of hiding from oneself a lack of faith.

Following on from this there is a need to continue the long Christian tradition of forming spaces in which we collectively invite, affirm, and celebrate this miracle that lies beyond the miraculous, beyond magic, beyond the sacred, and beyond the secular. We need to continue forming places that can render these ideas accessible at an immediate level, a level that does not depend upon the contingencies of one's education or the ability to think in abstract ways.

The question here is not "how do we make these ideas intelligible," for the miracle itself can be rendered intelligible only as unintelligible. What this means is that the miracle of faith is a happening, an event, that defies reduction to the realm of rational dissection. It can be known only as that which ruptures the sensible world of give and take, proportionality, and exchange, and is thus a truly supernatural phenomenon.

In contrast to forming a space that will make sense only to people who are highly educated, we must endeavor to form spaces that make sense to *nobody*, regardless of the level of education—spaces that rupture everyone and cause us all to rethink. Amidst the myriad religious communities that seek to be places that provide understanding, we need to form a space that takes this away, even if just for a few moments, so that something else can take place.

The point of such gatherings cannot be to offer some kind of occult, hidden truth that requires a certain level of education or intelligence. The idea of books such as this one is not to attempt to offer up the deep truth that is affirmed by Christianity, but rather to argue that no book could accomplish such a task— because that truth, if it exists at all, is not something that can be grasped as if it were a concept. Such a project, while it has a place, is in no way necessary for an encounter with that truth. The question then is how we can form collectives that seek to invite, affirm, recall, and relay this deep truth, not to provide a space where we try to understand it.

When writing about such spaces I will avoid using the word *church*, not because churches are excluded in any way from providing this space, but because the word can refer, in many people's minds, to the acceptance of a variety of doctrinal creeds, sacramental activities, and authority structures that are not necessary in the formation of these spaces. The type of space that I am referring to cannot be described as a new type of church, an alternative to church, an addition to church, or as a pathway that leads people back to church (although to those who attend it may legitimately act as one or more of these). So I will describe the type of collective that celebrates the miracle as a place of "transformance art."[87]

The point of transformance art is not simply to short-circuit our beliefs but, in doing so, to uncover and celebrate the truth that is affirmed in Christianity. It is not then a place of affirming the centrality of doubt but rather of exploring how an affirmation of religious doubt can help us to appreciate the indubitable event that may be housed within it.

In order to prepare people for an environment that is dedicated to exploring the miracle in a theatrical, ritualistic manner, it is useful to begin by creating projects that encourage individuals to question and rupture their belief system. In my own context we have developed a number of projects designed to facilitate this. These include "The Evangelism Project,"[88] "The Last Supper,"[89] "The Omega Course,"[90] and "Atheism for Lent."[91]

None of these are designed to change people's belief systems any more than they are designed to help solidify them. However, these outcomes may, and indeed sometimes do, happen. The main point of each of these projects is to introduce different perspectives on faith and life that help to expand our understanding and, more fundamentally, help the participant begin to reflect upon questions regarding what it means to affirm Christianity in the midst of complexity and doubt.

Theodrama

Once such projects are underway, the main challenge for practitioners concerns the development of a context that moves beyond such intellectually provocative environments toward something that allows us to reflect upon the miracle of faith, or rather reflect upon our faith in the miracle. Here I am referring to the formation of passionate, provocative gatherings, operating on the fringes of religious life, that offer anarchic experiments in theodrama that re-imagine the distinction between Christian and non-Christian, priest and prophet, doubt and certainty, the sacred and the secular—gatherings that employ a rich cocktail of music, poetry, prose, imagery, soundscapes, theatre, ritual, and reflection: gatherings that provide a place that is open to all, is colonized by none, and that celebrates diversity.

Such an immersive, theodramatic space would aim to affirm the need for (1) collective reflection; (2) a space where individuals can lay aside political, religious, and social identities; and finally (3) offer creative, ritualistic acts that invite, affirm, recall, and relate the event housed within the religion without religion that is Christianity.

In terms of providing a space for collective reflection, I am not referring to the development of a community with some central hierarchy that offers pastoral, financial, and spiritual support to those in need. Indeed often the most destructive element in the development of a community arises from the very statement that one is attempting to build a community. For what can so often happen is that those who need the most help join up in the hope that they will find support and encouragement. The result is that, for many fledgling groups, this places too high an emotional demand too early and leads to burnout.

To develop a healthy community, the best approach can actually involve being clear that one is not starting a community at all and that there will be no pastoral support, that no one will be charged with the job of taking in money and distributing it on people's behalf, and that no one will be responsible for calling you up if you stop attending events. In short, it must be clear that the group does not care about people's needs in the slightest. While this may sound deeply uncaring, the reason for stating this is precisely in order to help provide a healthy soil for real pastoral and financial support to grow.

Providing a space with no welcoming team or pastoral support group means that individuals need to take responsibility for welcoming and caring for others themselves. Here the role of those setting up the group is not to create a new priest/laity divide but rather to refuse to act in the role of a priest precisely so as to encourage a priesthood of all believers,[92] offering relational, mutually dependent, pastoral support. This does not mean that there is no place for leadership, for here the leader is the one who attempts to prevent any one person, including the leader, from taking over the space and taking on the role of some high priest. In such a space there is a radical refusal, by those who organize the gathering, to take on pastoral responsibility. For by refusing the place of power, the "pastors" equip everyone to be a pastor, simultaneously discouraging an unhealthy dependency in those who attend.

In this way we can focus on affirming our belonging together as equals in light of the event of faith. In maintaining a focus upon the miracle of faith, a context is thus created in which genuine relationships can develop and flourish. Instead of the de-politicized, privatized idea of a relationship involving two or more people looking toward one another while blocking out the world, here one provides the context for relationships in which people look out to a common horizon and as such enter into close proximity with others.

The second aspect of transformance art that I mention above relates to the formation of a space in which individuals can lay aside their various political, religious, and social identities for a time. Here I am referring to the formation of a space in which we place our various identities at the door for an hour in a theatrical performance of that Messianic vision of a time when all will be equal and all be bestowed with the same dignity. This is called a performance because it is not really possible to set aside our location in society, our political views, moral ideas, gender, sexual preferences, and so forth. But we can freely enter into a theatrical space in which we *act* as through there is neither Jew nor Greek, slave nor free, male nor female, employed nor unemployed, married nor unmarried, rich nor poor, oppressed nor oppressor. The hope here is that as we leave such a sacred place some element of this performance would remain with us, influencing our various identities in the world. For the various identities we have are themselves a performance. In philosophical terms this formation of a suspended position can be called the moment of *epoche*.

The third aspect of transformance art that I mention above concerns the development of creative, ritualistic acts that invite, affirm, recall, and relate the event housed within the religion without religion affirmed by Christianity.[93] There are any number of ways to do this, for the various spiritual practices of prayer, fasting, meditation, service to the poor, liturgy, baptism, communal singing, and anointing with oil, to name but a few, represent so many practices designed with this in mind. At their best, these practices are designed, not to reduce Christianity to a system, but rather to help us approach the central miracle of faith. Yet today so many of these practices have become mired in the project of an exclusivist, violent expression of Christianity and thus need to be renewed and rethought. This may mean that they are expressed in radically different ways than we would ever have expected and may go by very different names. But, at the end of the day, transformance art is simply a contemporary expression of what Christianity, as a religion without religion, has always been about, namely a set of passionate, provisional practices birthed from and responding to the earth-shattering undergoing of God.

The beauty of such communities is that the only treasure they have is one that can never be stolen but only shared. This is beautifully captured in a Zen parable concerning Master Ryokan. Ryokan was known to dwell at the foot of a great mountain in a humble dwelling. One day while he was out walking, a thief, who knew that no one lived near by and that Ryokan's house had no door, sneaked inside to steal the contents. But once inside the house he realized that there was nothing to steal. At that moment Ryokan returned to meet his startled guest. Saddened by what he saw, Ryokan said, "You have traveled so far to rob me and yet I have nothing for you; please take my clothes and blanket." With that Ryokan took off the clothes he was wearing and handed them to him along with the blanket he slept on. The thief, who was completely dumbfounded, grabbed the items and ran. When he had gone, Ryokan smiled as he lit a fire outside and considered the moon. "Poor man," he thought to himself, "if only he knew that I wanted to give him the moon."[94]

In this story the true treasure that Ryokan possessed was not something that could be stolen, because it was not something that Ryokan possessed. All one can do when one's treasure is of this nature is point toward it, recall it, and invite people to bask in it.

CONCLUSION
CONCLUSION

Crossing Out God for the Sake of God

Not long ago a piece of graffiti was sprayed onto a derelict building opposite the bar where we in ikon used to meet. It was nothing more than the word "God" with a circle around it and a line cutting through the circle from the top right to the bottom left (similar to a road sign, only crossing out *God*). We were deeply thankful for this anonymous gift, because it acted as such an insightful and thought-provoking entrance to our collective, providing a wonderful description of what transformance art is all about: denying God precisely to provide space for God; betraying our faith so as to remain faithful to it.

We began this short journey of words with the shadowy figure of Judas kissing his Messiah in the garden of Gethsemane and employed this as a means of posing the question as to whether it is possible, probable, or even necessary to betray our faith as a sign of our deep fidelity to it.

There is no doubt that the deepest betrayals must involve the love and trust of the one who has been betrayed, for to warrant the title of betrayal it must be carried out by one who has been given the power and position to do it. However, it is more difficult to see how the deepest betrayals can also demand the love of the one who carries it out. This word has been so negatively framed that it is now almost inextricably linked with terms such as *treachery*, *disloyalty*, and *duplicity*. Yet Christianity, as a religion without religion, would seem to demand that we be always prepared to betray our religious systems precisely so that holy water will never be detached from drinking water and communion bread never divorced from daily bread.

In conclusion, let us approach this idea of faithful betrayal via the following parable:

A Roman soldier had the legal right to demand that a citizen carry his pack for one mile as a service to the Empire. One day a small group of disciples who had embraced the way of Jesus early in his ministry heard him preaching by the side of a dusty road. They did not live with Jesus or the twelve, so they were excited to hear more of his teaching. As they listened, Jesus spoke: "The law says that you must carry a pack for one mile," he said to those gathered. "I say freely carry it for two."

The disciples were deeply impressed by these words, as it allowed for an opportunity to show the soldiers a hint of kingdom values and presented them with an opportunity to suffer in some small way for their faith.

As the practice of carrying a pack was common at the time, this small band of believers soon developed a reputation for their actions. Roman soldiers would often hope that the citizens they asked to carry their packs would be from among these disciples, and often a small bond of friendship would be sparked off between the soldiers and these followers of the Way.

After a year had passed, this custom had become so established in the life and works of this small group that it became a defining characteristic of shared life. The leaders would frequently refer to the teaching of Jesus and emphasize the need to carry a Roman soldier's pack for two miles as a sign of one's faith and commitment.

It so happened that Jesus heard about this community and, on his way to Jerusalem, stopped at their small meeting place. The leaders eagerly gathered together all the members of the group to hear what Jesus would wish to say to them. Once everyone had gathered, Jesus spoke: "Dear brothers and sisters, you are faithful and honest, but I have come to you with a second message, for you failed to understand the first one I offered. Your law says that you must carry a pack for two miles. I say carry it freely for three."

Here we witness an example of true faith giving birth to a system that must then be overturned. This idea of overturning Christianity is not something that became necessary at a certain point in time, as if it became a task only for those who came after the original disciples. Rather, Christianity's self-overcoming is a feature of the faith from its very inception. This act of overcoming was required from the very beginning and will continue without end or resolution until the very end. It is not that Christianity will ever be overcome, but rather that the Christian is one who must engage in a perpetual overcoming, embracing and rejecting at the same time. Hence the description of an authentic Christian as a non-Christian in the Christian sense of the term.

At various times throughout this book I have referred to the central happening of Christianity that sparks off this faithful betrayal in terms of Word, Event, Miracle, and Truth—all of which dwell beneath, before, and beyond objectification and thus are never rendered directly accessible to thought.

The concrete result of such ideas will continue to manifest in the development of subversive collectives that engage in creative acts of dis-course (discourse that send us off course) and that point toward, invite, and celebrate this unspeakable Happening. These temporary spaces will likely appear as much in art galleries, on street corners, in bars and basements, as they will in churches and cathedrals. They may involve rituals and creeds that have survived millennia, or they may have been dreamed up moments before they are acted out. The liturgies may be printed in hymnbooks or scrawled on the back of beer mats. They may be accompanied by angelic choirs or by someone beating out a rhythm on a battered, beer-soaked tabletop. They may be confessions of belief or affirmations of doubt. But everything, absolutely everything, will be designed to invite, encourage, solicit, seek out, recall, remember, reach out to, bow down before, and cry out to that unspeakable miracle testified to by faith—that miracle beyond miracle that dwells, quite literally, beyond belief.

ACKNOWLEDGMENTS

ACKNOWLEDGMENTS

When we enter the world we have no words, no language, no means of communication other than the most basic sounds. Our language is taught to us over time by those who have been speaking before we ever came onto the scene. It is through language that we, as subjects, come into existence, and it is through language that we are able to reflect upon the world that saturates us. Likewise, the words contained here have been received from others infinitely more experienced than I; they represent a rich mix of both gifts that have been received and spoils that have been stolen. And yet, like a child, I have mixed these words up in my own way and strived toward finding my own unique voice.

The task of writing the incommensurable is fraught with difficulties, for the very act would seem to betray it. However, in working though this problem I have benefited greatly from many who have walked this path before me. I am deeply grateful to my family for providing me with my first words, to thinkers such as John Caputo and Slavoj Žižek for helping to give me a language for this particular work, to ikon for offering the fires through which these words have been honed (particularly the cyndicate members Cary Gibson, Jonny McEwen, Michael Davis, Shirley Milburne, Jon Hatch, Jayne McConkey, Cazi, Willow, Kellie Turtle, Chris Fry, and Ben Jones) and to Jon Sweeney from Paraclete Press for giving me an opportunity to share these words with the wider world. I am also grateful to Michael Morrell, who helped with an early draft of this manuscript; Helena Macormac; and the various groups I have had the privilege to connect with this year. Of particular note is Aldea in Tucson, Arizona, where I finished the last pages of this book.

NOTES

NOTES

1. It is ironic that this phrase, which derives from the book *In His Steps* by Charles Sheldon, became such a financially lucrative and fashionable Christian accessory. Sheldon advocated a form of Christian activism known as the Social Gospel, and employed the phrase "in his steps" as a means of questioning what Jesus would do for the poor and marginalized in society.

2. It is only after Judas volunteers to commit the act that the Jewish authorities offer money—thus giving the impression that the money is more of a customary gift to say *thank you* rather than part of an exchange. See Mark 14:10–11.

3. Matthew 26:14–16.

4. Luke 22:3.

5. John 6:70.

6. Acts 1:15–19.

7. John 6:61–71.

8. See N.T. Wright, *Judas and the Gospel of Jesus* (Grand Rapids, MI: Baker Books, 2006), 43–48.

9. Matthew 27:3–8.

10. Mark 14:3–11.

11. John 13:18.

12.   Matthew 26:50 (italics mine).

13.   John 13:26–28.

14.   Matthew 26:24.

15.   For a good exploration of Judas see William Klassen, *Judas: Betrayer or Friend of Jesus?* (Minneapolis, MN: Augsburg Fortress Publishers, 2004).

16.   In addition to this, Judas sacrificed his reputation for all time by being labeled as the arch-enemy of Christ by most of the Christian Church.

17.   Slavoj Žižek, *The Puppet and the Dwarf* (Cambridge, MA: MIT Press, 2003), 16 (italics his).

18.   *The Gospel of Judas*, ed. Rodolphe Kasser, Marvin Meyer, and Gregor Wurst (Washington, D.C.: National Geographic, 2006), 43.

19.   Matthew 26:38.

20.   Indeed it is perhaps because of the very nature of the events themselves that we are left with writings that generate so many different accounts. Thus only by embracing all the accounts do we do justice to the relationship between Jesus and Judas.

21.   This is, of course, fictitious, except for the verse at the end which comes from John 12:23–25.

22.   Genesis 22:1–19.

23. These two stories are deeply complex, and the reasons for their existence in the Bible can be explained in a number of ways. For instance, one interpretation of the Abraham and Isaac story views it as a critique of child sacrifice rather than an endorsement of it. Here the author is seen to be getting on the right side of those who engage in this practice by showing

that even Abraham was prepared to engage in this sacrifice at the command of God. Then, once he had affirmed the faith and courage of those listening to or reading the story, the author then informs the audience that at the last minute God stops Abraham and says that a ram will be sufficient.

24. Genesis 18:20–21.

25. Genesis 32:28.

26. Acts 10:9–16.

27. Genesis 3:1–24.

28. The idea of God as a being who is unchanging, omnipotent, omniscient, and omnipresent and thus always right is more of a philosophical rendering than a biblical one. In metaphysical theology God is thought to be the perfect being, and perfection is related to the realm of total knowledge, total power, total presence, and absolute oneness. In contrast, the God we encounter in the Judeo-Christian Scriptures seems much more dynamic and messy.

29. Quoted from RSV in Ernest Bloch, *Atheism in Christianity: The Religion of the Exodus and the Kingdom*, trans. J.T. Swann (New York: Herder and Herder, 1972), 184.

30. It is ironic to note that a fundamentalist book entitled *Encylopedia of Bible Difficulties* written by Gleason L. Archer (Michigan: Zondervan, 1982) spends over four hundred and fifty pages offering answers to seeming problems and contradictions in the text. The sheer size of the book itself, which is still far from exhaustive, alongside the poorly honed explanations that are offered, does more to show the complex and conflictual nature of the text than any book designed to directly argue the case ever could.

31. Here I am indebted to the insights of Slavoj Žižek in *The Parallax View* (London: MIT Press, 2006).

32. Compare Matthew 3:1–3 with Luke 17:21.

33. Philippians 3:12–16.

34. Luke 17:20–21.

35. A nuclear shadow is formed as a result of the utter destruction of an object in a nuclear explosion. Because of the slight difference in heat, the place where the object once was is marked by a permanent shadow on the ground.

36. Or more accurately, between the two creation accounts that we find at the beginning of Genesis.

37. Compare Genesis 1:27 with Genesis 2:4–23.

38. The Midrash refers to a rich Hebraic tradition in which stories are written down that are inspired by elements of the Torah or that frame it in a different light. The Midrash is not given the same authority as the Torah but is employed as a means of exploring and interrogating the rich and diverse meanings of the Torah.

39. A term referring to the dark underworld of Kabbalistic imagination.

40. This name is constructed from the gathering together of every letter in the Torah to form a single word.

41. See Geraldine Pinch, *Egyptian Mythology: A Guide to the Gods, Goddesses, and Traditions of Ancient Egypt* (Oxford: Oxford University Press, 2002), 69–71, and the children's book *The Secret Name of Ra*, retold by Anne Rowe, illustrated by Donald Harley (Chicago, IL: Heinemann Library, 1996).

42. Exodus 3:4.

43. In chapter six we will examine the response that Moses is given and show how it can be viewed as a way of challenging this pursuit of the name.

44. Moses would have been well aware of the common names for God, such as the generic word "Elohim," which simply refers to God, and the unpronounceable Tetragrammaton, which is traditionally rendered as "LORD" in the Bible.

45. The Septuagint is a Greek rendering of Hebrew Scriptures from the third century BC. This document was the standard translation of the Old Testament in the early Christian church and is still viewed as canonical in the Eastern Orthodox tradition.

46. Exodus 3:14.

47. In reality he put forward a number of arguments. We will only be considering one here.

48. René Descartes, *Philosophical Writings,* ed. Elizabeth Anscombe and Peter Geach (London: Open University Press, 1970), 83.

49. Ibid., 85.

50. In chapter six I shall look at one of the problems with such an approach.

51. This view was deeply embedded in American evangelical theology in the thinking of Carl F. H. Henry, who believed that God's revelation was propositional in nature.

52. If this is the case then it seems to mean that as soon as one thinks about God (regardless of one's beliefs) one must, in order to be logical, assert that God exists.

53. Romans 12:1.

54. 1 John 4:8.

55. *Troy*, directed by Wolfgang Petersen (Warner Bros. Pictures, 2004).

56. Friedrich Nietzsche, *The Gay Science: With a Prelude in German Rhymes and an Appendix of Songs*, trans. Josefine Nauckhoff (Cambridge: Cambridge University Press, 2001), section 125.

57. René Descartes, "Fifth Replies," in *The Philosophical Writings of Descartes*, vol. 2, trans. John Cottingham et al. (Cambridge: Cambridge University Press, 1991), 253.

58. René Descartes and Thomas Hobbes, "Objections and Replies, the third set," in *Descartes: Philosophical Writings*, trans. Elizabeth Anscombe and Peter Thomas Geach (London: Nelson's University Press, 1971), 141 (italics his).

59. Blaise Pascal, *Penseés*, trans. A. J. Krailsheimer (New York: Penguin Books, 1995), 60.

60. Ibid.

61. Ibid., 60–61.

62. Ibid., 61.

63. Ibid., 63.

64. One of the most common translations/interpretations, as originally found in the Septuagint.

65. Everett Fox, trans., Schocken Bible, vol. 1, *The Five Books of Moses* (New York: Schocken Books, 1995).

66. Acts 9:1–9.

67. This is why there are so many different descriptions of God in the Bible and in the world. Each of these descriptions, when they arise from the undergoing of God, tells us something about God in the sense that the undergoing of God evokes this act. However, what one person thinks is the most beautiful

description of God may be violent and dangerous, because that person may have a damaged view of what is beautiful. Thus the violent fundamentalist cannot be dismissed as inauthentic; rather, the problem may simply be that the fundamentalist's view of what is most beautiful, a view that is inspired by the undergoing of God, is in fact destructive.

68. Mark 4:30–32.

69. Matthew 13:4.

70. This is a view that can be seen at work in the writing of people such as Josh McDowell and Francis Schaeffer.

71. Karl Marx, "Toward the Critique of Hegel's Philosophy of Right," in Karl Marx and Friedrich Engels, *Basic Writings of Politics and Philosophy*, ed. Lewis Feuer (New York: Anchor Books, 1959), 303.

72. For instance, in recent times we can recall thinkers such as Dietrich Bonhoeffer, Karl Barth, Jacques Ellul, Martin Luther King, Dorothy Day, Oscar Romero, Daniel Berrigan, and Gustavo Gutiérrez, to name but a few.

73. This distinction was first noted by the philosopher Gotthold Lessing and has been explored to some extent by philosophers such as David Flusser and, more recently, Giorgio Agamben.

74. John 9:25.

75. This is something that Ted Kluck and Kevin DeYoung accuse me of in the book *Why We're Not Emergent: By Two Guys Who Should Be* (Chicago: Moody Press, 2008), 49.

76. Luke 5:12–14.

77. Matthew 21:18–21.

78. Matthew 9:4–8.

79. Cf. John 9:1–34.

80. Matthew 16:13–20 (italics mine).

81. Is this not exactly what we see played out regularly when a high-profile religious leader is caught engaging in the very activity that he has constantly spoken out against? It would be premature to label this as a simple hypocrisy in which the person happily engages in an activity he says he rejects (the common line). Rather it is likely that he does reject his own behavior and that this rejection is the very fuel that drives him into it.

82. 1 Corinthians 6:12.

83. We can witness an extreme example of this when we consider the Nazi genocide. Most of those who helped to carry out the murders were not cruel and sadistic individuals. Rather, they were fed an ideological lie that openly acknowledged the horror of what they were doing. The ideology was offered in such a way that murder was seen as the moral act, an act that required the greatest ethical courage and strength to carry out. It was said that this murder was required in order to make Germany great again and lead it into a humane golden age. The genocide was then offered as the truly moral act, even though it was one that could never be spoken of. It was then the ideological system that helped to fuel the mass murder. Without it most of those involved could not have taken part in the genocide. The system itself allowed one to switch off from caring about the individual. Here the individual had to serve the ideological law rather than the law serving the individual.

84. We see this expressed throughout the text, for instance, Luke 15:1–32, or 1 Peter 2:9–10, where the excluded are included in the kingdom.

85. Ephesians 6:12.

86. Unpublished parable.

87. This insightful term was used in a review article dealing with *How (Not) to Speak of God* written by Gilo in *Movement* (2006) to describe the gatherings performed by ikon.

88. "The Evangelism Project" is designed to introduce people to the idea of being evangelized and thus rethinking what they believe. With this intent, this group makes regular visits to communities that are founded on certain beliefs about God, the world, and humanity that are likely to be different from those held by individuals in the group itself. The point is not to engage in some kind of interfaith dialogue but rather to listen, learn, and be open to being transformed by the encounter.

89. "The Last Supper" is a meeting in which twelve people gather together in an upper room over food and wine. Each evening a guest is invited to share what the guest believes and why he or she believes it. This is followed by a discussion around the themes that arise during the introduction. At the end of the night we decide how convinced we are by the guest and thus whether or not this will be the guest's last supper.

90. "The Omega Course" offers the tag line "exiting Christianity in twelve weeks" and is designed to provide a space for people to interrogate issues related to ideas such as the Virgin Birth, the deity of Jesus, the Atonement, the Resurrection, and the status of the Bible. The idea is to help all involved rethink their current theological positions, regardless of what they are, in light of exposure to other views.

91. "Atheism for Lent" is a yearly course that uses Lent as a time to reflect upon and discuss the most famous and

penetrating critiques of religion. Over the Lenten period we read the critiques of religion offered by people such as Nietzsche, Freud, and Marx, as well as some contemporary writers. Like "The Omega Course," this series is designed to help people rethink their theological commitments. However, this time the discussions relate to the views of thinkers from outside the Church rather than from within it.

92.   1 Peter 2:9; 1 Peter 2:4–5; Revelation 1:5–6, 5:6–10.

93.   On the ikon Web site (www.ikon.org.uk) there are some concrete examples of how we have ritualistically engaged in this process, or alternatively I have outlined ten examples of such gatherings in the book *How (Not) to Speak of God.*

94.   Adapted from Anthony DeMello, *Walking on Water,* ed. Gabriel Galache (New York: Crossroad Publishing, 1998), 28.

ABOUT PARACLETE PRESS

Who We Are

Paraclete Press is an ecumenical publisher of books and recordings on Christian spirituality. Our publishing represents a full expression of Christian belief and practice—from Catholic to Evangelical, from Protestant to Orthodox.

Paraclete Press is the publishing arm of the Community of Jesus, an ecumenical monastic community in the Benedictine tradition. As such, we are uniquely positioned in the marketplace without connection to a large corporation and with informal relationships to many branches and denominations of faith.

We like it best when people buy our books from booksellers, our partners in successfully reaching as wide an audience as possible.

What We Are Doing

Books

Paraclete Press publishes books that show the richness and depth of what it means to be Christian. Although Benedictine spirituality is at the heart of all that we do, we publish books that reflect the Christian experience across many cultures, time periods, and houses of worship.

We publish books that nourish the vibrant life of the church and its people—books about spiritual practice, formation, history, ideas, and customs.

We have several different series of books within Paraclete Press, including the best-selling Living Library series of modernized classic texts; A Voice from the Monastery—giving voice to men and women monastics about what it means to live a spiritual life today; award-winning literary faith fiction; and books that explore Judaism and Islam and discover how these faiths inform Christian thought and practice.

Recordings

From Gregorian chant to contemporary American choral works, our music recordings celebrate the richness of sacred choral music through the centuries. Paraclete is proud to distribute the recordings of the internationally acclaimed choir Gloriæ Dei Cantores, who have been praised for their "rapt and fathomless spiritual intensity" by *American Record Guide,* and the Gloriæ Dei Cantores Schola, which specializes in the study and performance of Gregorian chant. Paraclete is also the exclusive North American distributor of the recordings of the Monastic Choir of St. Peter's Abbey in Solesmes, France, long considered to be a leading authority on Gregorian chant performance.

Learn more about us at our Web site:
www.paracletepress.com,
or call us toll-free at 1-800-451-5006.